A Guide to Patent Applications

A Guide to Patent Applications

Francis E. LeVert

VAN NOSTRAND REINHOLD
New York

Library of Congress Catalog Card Number 92-24562
ISBN 0-442-01090-7

Printed in the United States of America

Van Nostrand Reinhold
115 Fifth Avenue
New York, New York 10003

Chapman and Hall
2–6 Boundary Row
London, SE1 8HN, England

Thomas Nelson Australia
102 Dodds Street
South Melbourne 3205
Victoria, Australia

Nelson Canada
1120 Birchmount Road
Scarborough, Ontario M1K 5G4, Canada

16 15 14 13 12 11 10 9 8 7 6 5 4 3 2 1

Library of Congress Cataloging-in-Publication Data

LeVert, Francis E., 1939–
A guide to patent applications / Francis E. LeVert.
p. cm.
Includes bibliographical references and index.
ISBN 0-442-01090-7
1. Patent practice—United States—Popular works. 2. Patent laws and legislation—United States—Popular works. I. Title.
KF3120.Z9L48 1992
346.7304'86—dc20 92-24562
[347.306486] CIP

To my family—Faye, Francis, Gerald, and Lisa.

Contents

Preface

Independent inventors (apart from large corporations) have always contributed a great deal to the technological progress of the United States. Perhaps you are such a person. If so, you are part of a group of people who will continue to create as many important inventions in the future as you have in the past. As part of that group, you may often be puzzled by such problems as whether to seek patent protection and what steps to take to get the benefit of patent law. You have basically two choices:

- Guide the idea from the point of conception to a patent issued by the U.S. Patent Office.
- Turn to a professional for aid in protecting the invention.

In either case, you must understand the steps to take from the point of conception to the issuance of a patent by the U.S. Patent and Trademark Office (PTO).

There are generally two driving forces behind invention:

- A pressing need for a device, material, or process to perform some function.
- Efforts that are relevant outside the immediate context that gave them birth.

An example of the latter may be a machining technique invented to provide a precision part for manufacturing optical instruments that may find applications in the watch-making industry. An example of the former is the manual automobile pusher invented by a Chicago resident (me) to push his automobile out of snow ruts during the severe 1978 winter.

It is probably safe to venture that hundreds of useful tools invented by people like this Chicagoan never go through the patent process. Some inventors who do think of applying for a patent are probably dissuaded by others or deterred because of the expense involved in employing professional help. Still others know the odds against their idea being brought to the marketplace and, therefore, make no attempts to secure a patent.

Fortunately, there exists a class of inventors who persevere against these odds. Progress and the quality of life depend on these individuals, and it is their inventions and innovations, great and not so great, that have revolutionized our lives. For as Sir Alexander Fleming stated, "It is the lone worker who makes the first advance in a subject: the details may be worked out by a team, but the prime idea is due to the enterprise, thought and perception of an individual."

The well-known inventor Jacob Robinow expressed the same sentiments as he addressed an inventor workshop held in Atlanta, Georgia, in October 1980. In praise of the independent inventor, he cited a short list of great innovations, which included:

- Atomic energy
- The computer
- Xerography
- The laser
- Microwave and radar technology

The first advances in each of these innovations were primarily due to the efforts of lone workers.

Most inventors are, on the average, well served by company patent agents or attorneys who are skilled at assessing patentability and getting the broadest claim coverage for the invention. Recognizing this fact, I am directing this book to the needs of independent inventors who, because of either need or desire, prefer to write their own claims and perform their own patent searches. It is the outgrowth of several years fraught with both disappointing and satisfying encounters with the U.S. PTO as I tried to prosecute my own applications. Because I developed its substance using my trial-and-error experiences, the book embodies those problems most likely to be encountered by a layperson in prosecuting patent applications.

I believe that, like myself, many inventors do not work on (or reduce to practice) many innovations that would be beneficial to humankind, simply because of the expense involved in securing a patent. I also believe that an inventor can, through diligence and practice, write a set of claims that will provide adequate protection for an invention. I assume that a fraction of the 99 percent perspiration Thomas Edison spoke of (when he said "Genius is one percent inspiration and 99 percent perspiration") can be spent in writing one's own patent application.

A Guide to Patent Applications follows the order of my maturation in the art of patenting. Chapters 1 through 3 discuss my experiences in the invention/innovation process, including a recounting of all my initial encounters with the U.S. PTO—from the point of submission of my first application to the issuance of my first patent. This portion of the book is a kind of "lessons learned" presentation. It embodies many of the problems encountered by the novice in attempting to patent an invention without benefit of a lawyer.

While pursuing my first application, I discovered the importance of keeping good records and the need for a thorough prior art search. Chapters 2 and 3 discuss these two processes.

Once you decide to pursue an idea to an allowed patent, you will probably wonder about patentability and the protection provided you by a patent. Chapters 4, 5, and 6 deal with the question of patentability, the various patent codes that are important to know, and the parts of a patent. Because the patent's claims *are* your invention, I give them particular attention. In Chapter 6, I discuss the details of how you apply for protection for your idea in a foreign country or countries.

Chapter 7 discusses the innovation process and the reasons why many inventions are never commercialized. Chapter 8 considers ways to protect the property rights afforded you by an issued patent.

Taking an idea from conceptualization, to allowance of a patent, to commercialization is a difficult road. This book provides the map for that journey if you are strong-hearted enough to take it. The path is not without its potential pitfalls—nor, am I reminded, is the path to completing a finished manuscript. I would like to thank Francis and Faye LeVert, S. Moore, and K. McMaster for helping me avoid those pitfalls. Their assistance is greatly appreciated.

A Guide to Patent Applications

1

A Case History of a Novice

How did I happen to write this book? My own first experience at applying for a patent by myself, coupled with the uncertainties and frustrations I encountered even after reading the available books on the subject, convinced me of the need for it. My eventual success in obtaining patents assured me that I had acquired the necessary knowledge to help others gain this skill.

I was introduced to the art of writing my own patent application while employed at Argonne National Laboratory, where I coinvented three radiation monitoring devices. A patent attorney assigned to our case discussed the process with me. I was intrigued. The attorney encouraged me. I decided to try my hand at getting myself a patent.

I certainly was not going to hazard getting a defective patent on something I thought commercially valuable, but I did have a cornball idea I was willing to expend. So I was ready for a maiden voyage into patenting.

I recommend this strategy to every nonprofessional on a first attempt at writing a patent application. It does not threaten your money-making ideas, and the written encounter with the U.S. Patent and Trademark Office (PTO) will provide a very important learning experience. The body of the patent and, most important, the claims, will be examined by a professional patent attorney in the U.S. PTO, and will be rejected if seriously flawed.

1.1 THE IDEA AND INVENTION STAGE

The idea for my first patent application was born during the Chicago winter of 1978. Snow inundated the city in a short period of weeks. The city could keep only the major through-streets reasonably passable. Parking areas on residential streets stayed filled with two to three feet of snow, untouched by snow-removal equipment. Tremendous ice traps developed on these side streets when cars plowed over the snow. Travel on them was treacherous. Exiting from one's driveway became an act of courage. Getting stuck was routine.

Like everyone else, I rocked my car by shifting from first to reverse and vice versa, until the car inched free. Or I solicited the help of a neighbor to push it into the streets. I wanted something easier, less dangerous to my automobile's life and to my own. Heart attacks were not infrequent among the aged automobile pushers. So it occurred to me that a manual device, with some mechanical advantage, capable of pushing an automobile out of ice and snow ruts, would be useful.

A need was defined, and an idea was born! I soon had an invention that was practical and set about actually making the device, which liberated me from my driveway before the snow-removal teams made Chicago side streets passable again.

1.2 A STATE-OF-THE-ART SEARCH

After I had made the prototype of the manual automobile pusher and used it successfully to free several of my neighbors' cars, someone suggested that I patent it. Because of my experience with patents at Argonne National Laboratory, I knew that I needed to find out what kind of manual pushers existed in the marketplace. I decided first on a preliminary review of several popular mechanic and automobile magazines to determine the novelty of the device. I found nothing commercially available that looked like my invention or performed the pushing function in a manner similar to it; that is, I found no "prior art" advertised in these magazines. Just because something is not being sold on the open market, however, does not mean that it has not been patented. This is a lesson learned by many inventors after costly investments of time and money.

The term prior art is widely used, and you need to be aware of its meaning. I will discuss it more in detail in Chapter 3, to make it clear. For the moment, suffice it to say that prior art is knowledge generally known or published.

My next step, therefore, was to consult the *Manual of Patent Classification* and the *Official Gazette of the U.S Patent and Trademark Office*. I found the *Gazette* in the Chicago Public Library. It would be a slight understatement of my first foray into the stacks of the Chicago Public Library to say that it was not easy! In fact, I made several mistakes in this first search. However, even with my mistakes, I identified two pertinent inventions:

- Patent number 3,029,065, issued April 10, 1962 to C. Buddingh, entitled "Means for Moving Vehicles."
- Patent number 3,099,435, issued July 30, 1963 to C. C. Nixon, entitled "Bumper Jack Pusher Extension."

I have included copies of these patents in Appendix E. You may find it helpful to review these patents in light of the examiner's remarks (which are presented later in this chapter) concerning my patent application. In Chapter 2, I shall describe, step by step, how to search for prior patents.

A careful review of the patents of Buddingh and Nixon convinced me that my automobile pusher was novel. My belief in the "novelty" of my invention was supported by the fact that the patents of Buddingh and Nixon did not reveal devices that operated in the same way as mine, even though they achieved the same results.

In addition to the claims of the prior art (i.e., the patents of Buddingh and Nixon), I also studied the description and mode of operation of the devices presented in the specifications of these patents. In both cases, I thought the inventions were different from mine. I later learned that my invention had to be more than just different from the prior art—it had to be different in ways that were substantial and significant.

Most of the time you will find at least one patent that discloses an invention that is very similar to yours. After studying the patents, I convinced myself that the design and the operation of my pusher were not obvious extensions of the Nixon and Buddingh devices; that is, I felt that I had made *nonobvious* improvements in this art.

My invention was an improvement, then, on the art of automobile pushers. Others had worked on mechanical ways to move an automobile, and my invention was simply a refinement of those devices. The concept, hence, was not new, and I had already discovered that a preliminary search had been valuable. I had uncovered at least two inventors with what appeared to be workable ideas for manual automobile pushers. But most important, I had learned that, at best, I could get a patent only with very narrow claims. My claims had to be limited to the elements that described the specific design or structure of my pusher.

I studied the prior art in depth and decided that both inventions taught the use of attachments for the ordinary bumper jack in order to turn it into a manual automobile pusher. However, although both inventions could adequately perform the function provided by my invention, the invention was sufficiently novel and useful to warrant the submission of a patent application.

Inventors, by their very drive to invent, will probably fall in love with their ideas. By the time an inventor has spent some time developing an idea, it can become a passion. The search for prior art has a proper cooling effect on one's perspective. If you know that prior art exists without having changed the business world, the invention may not be as significant as you would like to think. You may need to prepare yourself for this development. Unless your invention has an appealing advantage over those earlier efforts, the patent you get (by a lot of further effort) may provide only a convenient conversation piece and a cover for an unsightly blemish on the den wall.

You may, as I did, use the process as a means of sharpening your skills. Then you will be ready to write an application for a future idea that will be commercially viable and will not have been anticipated by countless inventors of record. You may be better served to study my mistakes, understand the rules and requirements set forth in this book, and use that information to improve the patent you get via a professional. I have reproduced portions of the original application here as an object lesson. The claims and the patent drawing submitted are shown in Figures 1-1 and 1-2, respectively. The contents of the full application, as an issued patent, are given in Appendix E.

1.3 DISCUSSION OF MY FIRST OFFICE ACTION

The response of an examiner to a patent application is called an office action.

I sent my application via registered mail to: The Commissioner of Patents and Trademarks, Washington, D.C., 20231. Although the cost of sending the application as registered mail was small compared to the cost for processing the application in the PTO, I learned later that this action was unnecessary, and I simply could have included a "certificate of mailing" with my application. Appendix A shows the acceptable format for a certificate of mailing letter (Form 7).

I waited for the result of this application. When it came, the action did not contain any real surprises other than the fact that it was not rejected outright by the Patent Office. I received the material you see in Figures 1-3, 1-4, and 1-5. These are the examiner's responses, his first action on my application. Typically, you will not have to wait longer than 14 months for these responses.

From Figure 1-3, you will see that the examiner's first action was to reject all three claims and to allow me a three-month statutory period to reply to his action. In Figure 1-4, the examiner cited all the relevant references found in his search. Figure 1-5 indicates the problems with the drawing submitted with the original application. The drawings for the application (see Figure 1-2) must be made in India ink on 8.5" × 14" two- or three-ply bristol board, and must have a 2" margin at the top and a 0.25" margin at both sides and the bottom. The drawing given in Figure 1-2 was not what I sent to the PTO in my first application. What I sent was done with India ink, but on clear

The embodiments of the invention in which an exclusive property or privilege is claimed are defined as follows:

1. A manual automobile pusher capable of extricating an immobile automobile from an ice, snow or mud rut, the manual automobile pusher comprising: Means for making firm contact with either the front or rear bumper of an automobile; means for adjusting the vertical angle at which contact with an automobile bumper is made; means for transmitting a force to an automobile through displacement of a rigid member; means for generating the transmitted force; means for determining the size and direction of displacement of a rigid member; means for making high friction contact with surface that supports said automobile; and means for providing structural strength to said manual automobile pusher when it is in use.

2. A device for freeing automobiles from ice, snow or mud ruts, the device comprising: a rubber cradle; a metal cradle; a curved hollow rectangular metal sleeve connected to the metal cradle by a smooth steel pivot pin; a ratchet mechanism connected to the curved hollow rectangular metal sleeve; a curved solid metal rack post with identical radius of curvature as said hollow rectangular metal sleeve designed to mate with the mechanism; a metal rectangular base connected to the curved rack post by a smooth steel pivot pin; a set of metal studs mounted on the metal rectangular base to prevent slippage; a telescoping metal strut connected to both said metal rectangular base and to said hollow rectangular metal sleeve by a smooth steel pin; a spring-loaded mechanism mounted on said telescoping metal strut; a hand-operated lever with two positions to engage or disengage the spring-loaded mechanism.

3. The device of this invention wherein the drive mechanism comprises a worm gear with the rack modified to accept such a driving mechanism.

FIGURE 1-1. The Introduction to and the Claims of My First Application

tracing paper. As you see, in Figure 1-5, this cost me an additional $10.00, plus the time spent remaking the drawing.

Accompanying the rejection form was the examiner's written explanation for rejecting the patent application, shown in Figure 1-6.

The first paragraph of the examiner's response is tantamount to a formality. The examiners advise all applicants who submit applications without using an attorney that maximum protection for an invention can best be had through a practicing attorney.

Although I did not find this response to my first application reassuring, when I reread the application itself, I could see the correctness of the examiner's argument. The second paragraph is particularly substantive; it indicates the important point that *no new matter can be introduced in the claims.* In other words, nothing that was not described in the Description of the Invention and clearly illustrated in the drawings can be introduced in the

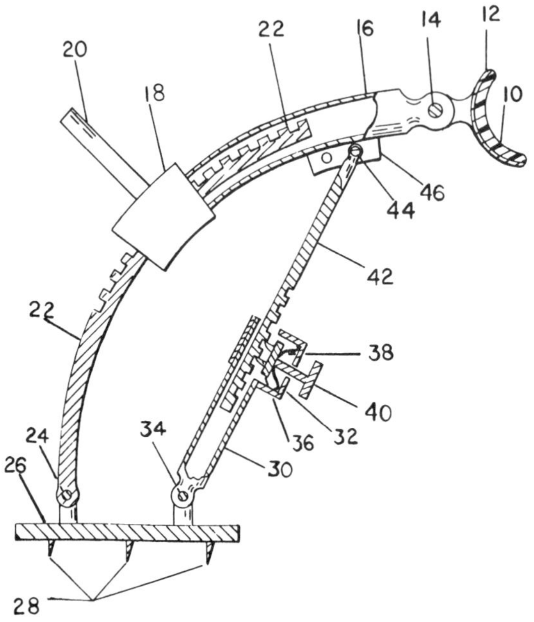

FIGURE 1-2. My First Patent Drawing

Claims. I had mentioned the worm gear/rack post structure in the Detailed Description of the Invention, but because it was not shown in the drawing, the examiner regarded it as new matter. In the third paragraph, the examiner cites *35 U.S.C.112*, which, as we shall see later in Chapter 4, requires that the specification of the invention be described fully in clear, concise, and exact terms.

In the fourth paragraph of this discourse, the reason is given for the rejection of Claim 1. It is *35 U.S.C. 102*! (See Section 4.2.2 of Chapter 4.) Here the examiner stated his most important objection to my invention. It was that the prior art he cited anticipated the proposed invention. A review of the claims of Fotheringham (see his patent reproduced in Appendix E) showed me how similar were several of the means he described to those of my own application.

I learned that what I had done was typical of the nonprofessional. Nonprofessionals have a tendency to be too broad, and hence vague, in their claims. They seek the most protection for their inventions and lose credibility.

As I reconsidered, I saw that the means evident in Claim 1 were incorrect, given the prior art that I already knew existed. I had written them with the intention of trying to avoid easy circumvention of my patent. Ideally, I now

UNITED STATES DEPARTMENT OF COMMERCE
Patent and Trademark Office

Address : COMMISSIONER OF PATENTS AND TRADEMARKS
Washington, D.C. 20231

SERIAL NUMBER	FILING DATE	FIRST NAMED APPLICANT	ATTORNEY DOCKET NO.
011,174	02/09/79	Francis E. Le Vert	None

Francis E. Le Vert
7233 South Luella
Chicago, Ill. 60649

MAILED
JAN 15 1980
U.S. PATENT AND TRADEMARK OFFICE

EXAMINER	
ART UNIT	PAPER NUMBER
323	4

DATE MAILED:

This is a communication from the examiner in charge of your application.

COMMISSIONER OF PATENTS AND TRADEMARKS

[X] This application has been examined. [ ] Responsive to communication filed on ________ [ ] This action is made final.

A shortened statutory period for response to this action is set to expire 3 month(s), ______ days from the date of this letter.
Failure to respond within the period for response will cause the application to become abandoned. 35 U.S.C. 133

Part I THE FOLLOWING ATTACHMENT(S) ARE PART OF THIS ACTION:

1. [X] Notice of References Cited, Form PTO-892.
2. [X] Notice of Informal Patent Drawing, PTO-948.
3. [X] Notice of Informal Patent Application, Form PTO-152.
4. [ ] ________

Part II SUMMARY OF ACTION

1. [X] Claims 1-3 are pending in the application.

   Of the above, claims ________ are withdrawn from consideration

2. [ ] Claims ________ have been cancelled.
3. [ ] Claims ________ are allowed.
4. [X] Claims 1-3 are rejected.
5. [ ] Claims ________ are objected to.
6. [ ] Claims ________ are subject to restriction or election requiremen
7. [ ] The formal drawings filed on ________ are acceptable.
8. [ ] The drawing correction request filed on ________ has been [ ] approved. [ ] disapproved.
9. [ ] Acknowledgment is made of the claim for priority under 35 U.S.C. 119. The certified copy has [ ] been received. [ ] not been received. [ ] been filed in parent application, serial no. ________ , filed on ________ .
10. [ ] Since this application appears to be in condition for allowance except for formal matters, prosecution as to the merits is closed in accordance with the practice under Ex parte Quayle, 1935 C.D. 11; 453 O.G. 213.
11. [ ] Other

PTOL-326 (rev. 10-78)

FIGURE 1-3. Examiner's First Action

FORM PTO-46-42 (REV. 12-76) (FORMERLY PTO-892) — U.S. DEPARTMENT OF COMMERCE PATENT AND TRADEMARK OFFICE	SERIAL NO.	GROUP ART UNIT	ATTACHMENT TO PAPER NUMBER
NOTICE OF REFERENCES CITED	011,174	323	10
	APPLICANT (S): Le Vert		

U.S. PATENT DOCUMENTS

•		DOCUMENT NO.	DATE	NAME	CLASS	SUB-CLASS	FILING DATE IF APPROPRIATE
	A	4129286	12/12/78	Anell	254	103	2/3/77
	B	1821627	9/31	Fotheringham	254	126	2/14/29
	C	3029065	4/10/62	Buddingh	254	35	1/15/60
	D	3099435	7/30/63	NIXON	254	35/135R	6/19/61
	E	1325964	12/23/19	Templeton	254	109	3/4/18
	F						
	G						
	H						
	I						
	J						
	K						

FOREIGN PATENT DOCUMENTS

•		DOCUMENT NO.	DATE	COUNTRY	NAME	CLASS	SUB-CLASS	PERTINENT SHTS. DWG	PERTINENT PP. SPEC.
	L								
	M								
	N								
	O								
	P								
	Q								

FIGURE 1-4. Notice of References Cited

realize, Claim 2 should have been the basic all-encompassing claim, with all dependent claims built upon it. The examiner's statement that Claim 3 lacked dependency meant that Claim 3 should have referred, in this case, to the independent Claim 2. A review of the patents in Appendix E will illustrate this point very clearly. Notice that all dependent claims refer to an independent claim. (I will discuss claims in more detail in Chapter 5.)

I was pleased, however, to see that my search of the prior art had followed the lines of the examiner's. He cited two of the patents I had identified as prior art (i.e., those of Nixon and Buddingh). Before I responded to the examiner's first action, I arranged a telephone interview with him. The purpose of the interview was to find out from him what was required to make

FORM PTO-948
REV. 7-78)

U. S. DEPARTMENT OF COMMERCE
Patent and Trademark Office

Attachment to paper no.

S.N.

NOTICE OF INFORMAL PATENT DRAWINGS

The drawings in this application are objected to by the Draftsman as informal for the reason(s) checked below:

1. [x] Lines Pale.
2. [ ] Paper Poor.
3. [ ] Numerals Poor.
4. [ ] Lines Rough and Blurred.
5. [ ] Shade Lines Required.
6. [ ] Figures Must be Numbered.
7. [ ] Heading Space Required.
8. [ ] Figures Must Not be Connected.
9. [ ] Criss – Cross Hatching Objectionable.
10. [ ] Double–Line Hatching Objectionable.
11. [ ] Parts in Section Must Be Hatched.
12. [ ] Solid Black Objectionable.
13. [ ] Figure Legends Placed Incorrectly.
14. [ ] Mounted Photographs.
15. [ ] Extraneous Matter Objectionable (Rule 84 (1)).
16. [x] Other

A. [x] The estimated cost for correcting the above informalities is $ 10 . Order for correction is required in a separate letter to the Draftsman. Other changes if any, may require an additional fee.

B. [ ] New drawings are required and can be prepared by the Draftsman at an estimated cost of $________.

If applicant provides the new drawings a comparison fee of $10.00 is required.

C. [ ] New drawings are required from applicant together with a comparison fee of $10.00. The Patent and Trademark Office Drafting Division cannot prepare these drawings at the present time.

To ensure prompt processing and forwarding of new drawings to the examiner, each sheet should include the Serial Number and Group Art Unit in the upper right corner within 3/4" of the top edge of the paper.

NOTE: Where use of a deposit account is authorized for payment for the required corrections or for new drawings, two copies of such authorization are required.

FIGURE 1-5. Notice of Informal Patent Drawings on My First Application

An examination of this application reveals that applicant is unfamiliar with patent prosecuting procedure. While an inventor may prosecute his application himself, his lack of skill in this field usually acts as a liability in affording him maximum protection for his invention. Applicant is advised to secure the services of a registered patent attorney or agent to further prosecute the application for him, since the value of a patent is largely dependent upon the skillful preparation and prosecution thereof. The Office cannot aid in selecting an attorney or agent.

The drawing is objected to under 37 C.F.R. 1.83. All features that are claimed must be clearly illustrated. The worm gear rack post structure of Claim 3 is omitted from the drawings. If a claim is retained to this feature, such subject matter is required to be illustrated.

Claims 1-3 are rejected as failing to define the invention in the manner required by 35 U.S.C.112. In Claim 1, it is not clear what structure is capable of providing a 'means for determining the size of displacement'... and it is not clear what means provides 'structural strength.' In Claim 3 the claim dependency is omitted.

Insofar as the claims can be understood, Claim 1 is rejected under 35 U.S.C. 102 as being anticipated by Fotheringham. The various recited means are found to have equivalents in Fotheringham.

Anell is cited to show a similar lever lifting structure. Nixon and Buddingh are cited to show various car pusher jacks. Templeton is cited to show a pivoting base with ground engaging teeth, Bryant et al. is cited to show a curved rack used for a jacking purpose.

FIGURE 1-6. Examiner's Response to My First Patent Application

an amendment to the case in response to the first office action. Figure 1-7 shows an example of the written examiner interview summary that an examiner must include in the file each time that he interacts with an applicant. This record should include a brief identification of the general thrust of the principal arguments presented to the examiner. It, along with all the office actions and the inventor's responses, becomes a part of the official file of transactions associated with an application. This file is called a file wrapper.

1.4 HOW I RESPONDED TO THE FIRST OFFICE ACTION ON MY FIRST PATENT APPLICATION

When I received my first office action, I was, as indicated above, somewhat overwhelmed and just a little bit proud that I had done something right—the search had been on track. The top of Figure 1-3 shows that I was allowed the standard statutory period of three months to respond to the examiner's actions. Although this appears to be a long time, you will, as I did, discover that it is not enough in light of the knowledge that the examiner will summarily reject the application (i.e., send you a final office action) if he

UNITED STATES DEPARTMENT OF COMMERCE
Patent and Trademark Office
Address: COMMISSIONER OF PATENTS AND TRADEMARKS
Washington, D.C. 20231

SERIAL NUMBER	FILING DATE	FIRST NAMED APPLICANT	ATTORNEY DOCKET NO.
11,174	02-09-79	FRANCIS E. LEVERT	

EXAMINER	
ART UNIT	PAPER NUMBER
323	5

DATE MAILED:

EXAMINER INTERVIEW SUMMARY RECORD

All participants (applicant, attorney, agent) representing applicant:

(1) MR. LeVert, applicant (3) ______

(2) ______ (4) ______

Date of interview Oct 1, 1979

Type: [✓] Telephonic [ ] Personal (copy is given to applicant).

Exhibit shown or demonstration conducted: [ ] Yes [✓] No.

Agreement [✓] was reached with respect to some or all of the claims in question. [✓] was not reached.

Claims discussed: 1 - 3

Identification of prior art discussed: art of record

Description of the general nature of what was agreed to if an agreement was reached, or any other comments:

Answered applicant's questions regarding what would be necessary to make an amendment to the case in response to first office action, Applicant advised of what would be nesessary for a fully responsive amendment.

(A fuller necessary description and any available copy of amendments that the examiner agreed would render the claims allowable, or where no copy of the amendments is available, a summary thereof, is attached.)

[✓] It is not necessary for applicant to supplement the information on this form or to submit a separate record of the substance of the interview.

APPLICANTS, ATTORNEYS AND AGENTS ARE REMINDED OF THEIR RESPONSIBILITY TO SUPPLEMENT THIS RECORD WITH AN INDICATION OF THE SUBSTANCE OF THE INTERVIEW AS REQUIRED BY 37 CFR 1.133(b) AND SECTION 713.04 OF THE MANUAL OF PATENT EXAMINING PROCEDURE. (See reverse side for text of Section 713.04.)

PTOL-413 (rev. 9/78)

APPLICANT'S COPY

FIGURE 1-7. Record of My Telephone Interview with the Examiner of My First Application considers your reply nonresponsive. Failure to answer the examiner's objections will terminate the process.

Each response to an examiner's office action must have the form shown in Figure 1-8. The lines where you wish to make changes in your application must be identified and the proposed amendment(s) clearly stated. This process will make responses to Office Actions much more convenient and reduce the possibility of the examiner misinterpreting any changes you wish to make in the application.

Applicant: Francis E. LeVert

Serial No: 11,174 Group Art Unit: 323

Filed: February 9, 1979 Examiner:

For: Manual Automobile Pusher

Amendment

The Commissioner of Patents and Trademarks
Washington, D.C. 20231

Sir:

In response to the Office Action of August 29, 1979, it is requested that the above - entitled application be amended as follows:

In the Detailed Description of the Invention:

Page 5, line 29, between the words "smooth" and the numeral "44" delete the phrase "steel cap screw" and insert "pivot pin."

In the Claims:

Claim 1, delete lines 10 and 11; that is, the statement "Means for determining the size and direction of displacement of a rigid member."

Claim 1, delete lines 14 and 15 in Claim 1; that is, the statement "Means for providing structural strength to said manual automobile pusher when it is in use."

Claim 2, line 5, insert between the words "connected" and "to" the phrase "with non-slippage contact." Insert a semi-colon after "pin" on line 6 and the word "steel" for "steep." Also, delete the words "with ... other" beginning on line 6 and lasting through line 8.

FIGURE 1-8. My Response to the Examiner's First Action

Claim 2, line 18, delete the word "pin" and insert the word "pins." Insert a semi-colon ";" after "pins" on line 18. Delete the entire line 19, "and a cap screw, respectively."

Claim 3, please delete Claim 3.

Response to Examiner Rejections

The examiner has rejected claims 1-3 under 35 U.S.C. 102 "as being anticipated by Fotheringham." Fotheringham (U.S. Patent 1,821,827) describes a lifting jack, which is designed for lifting motor cars and similar vehicles. This applicant believes that Fotheringham's invention does not anticipate applicant's invention in that it is designed primarily for pushing vehicles. Fotheringham's invention transmits force in one direction, while the applicant's invention provides both lifting and pushing forces (i.e., forces in two directions).

In Claim 1, line 5, applicant claims that the vertical angle at which contact is made with the bumper of an automobile can be adjusted, thereby generating a vertical component (lifting force) of the applied force zero. This kind of transmitted force was not anticipated by Fotheringham. Further, Fotheringham's invention cannot be used for pushing.

Remarks

The applicant has diligently tried to be responsive to the rejections put forth by the Examiner. The applicant appreciates the detailed and clear basis for the Examiner's rejections of the claims as presented by him and has endeavored to present the new set of claims in a clear and definite manner.

Respectfully submitted,

F.E. LeVert
Feb. 5, 1980

FIGURE 1-8. *(continued)*

1.5 DISCUSSION OF MY SECOND OFFICE ACTION

The examiner was not persuaded by arguments for the novelty of my invention put forth in Figure 1-8, as witnessed by his response repeated below.

The Examiner's Second Action, in response to my request for amendments to my original application, was as follows:

> Claim 2 is rejected under *35 U.S.C. 112* as failing to distinctly claim an invention. No structural correlation between the "rubber cradle" and "metal cradle" is recited in the claim.
>
> Claim 1 is rejected under *35 U.S.C. 103* as being unpatentable over Fotheringham in view of Stickle. At least three different means are provided in Fotheringham for adjusting the vertical angle at which the device engages on an automobile bumper. The mere inclusion of a "high friction contact means" would be obvious in view of Stickle (see element 21 in Stickle).
>
> Claim 2 will be allowed if amended to obviate the *35 U.S.C. 112* rejection.

Notice that something new has been added. The examiner has added the patent of Stickle (see Appendix E) as being anticipating art. But he admits the possibility of allowing Claim 2 if I can overcome the rejection under *35 U.S.C. 112.* I established the structural correlation he referred to by changing the fourth line of Claim 2 to make the structural connection between the rubber and metal cradles.

The fact that the examiner introduced the patent of Stickle caused me some concern for two reasons:

- This development illustrated that a patentability search by the patent office may not reveal all the pertinent patents.
- The complexities of the process were becoming evident.

That is, the PTO may grant a patent for an invention even though it has been anticipated by prior art.

The claim I was finally allowed is as follows:

2. A device for freeing automobiles from ice, snow, or mud ruts, the device comprising: a rubber cradle; *a metal cradle connected to the rubber cradle*; a curved hollow rectangular metal sleeve connected with nonslippage contact to the metal cradle as by a smooth steel pivot pin; a ratchet mechanism connected to the curved hollow rectangular metal sleeve; a curved solid metal rack post with identical radius of curvature as said hollow rectangular metal sleeve designed to mate with the mechanism; a metal rectangular base connected to the curved rack post by a smooth steel pivot pin; a set of metal studs mounted on the metal rectangular base

to prevent slippage; a telescoping metal strut connected to both said metal rectangular base and to said hollow rectangular metal sleeve by a smooth steel pin; a spring-loaded mechanism mounted on said telescoping metal strut; a hand-operated lever with two positions to engage or disengage the spring-loaded mechanism.

This claim is identical to the earlier Claim 2 except where italicized.

The italicized (for emphasis here) phrase provides the structural correlation between the rubber and metal cradles. I do not represent this claim as a model claim. I use it only to illustrate the process. This claim has too many elements and too much structural specificity. The discussion in Chapter 5 makes many of the shortcomings of this claim obvious.

The drawings must meet certain standards. Mine obviously did not. The shading of lines was not consistent. They were pale in some places, as indicated in Figure 1-5.

My response was to redo the figure and resubmit it to the Chief Draftsman of the U.S. PTO. All figure changes must be submitted to the Chief Draftsman. Table 1-1 presents some general requirements that you should meet for drawings. The rules and guidelines of the PTO for drawings are presented in a condensed form in Appendix D. I failed to meet most of these requirements with my first application.

1.6 WHAT TO DO IF YOUR RESPONSE TO AN OFFICE ACTION IS REJECTED

If your response (i.e., your first amendment to your application) to the first office action does not place the application in condition for allowance (issue of a patent), the next time you hear from the examiner will be, in most cases, in the form of a final office action. If the examiner cites new references, you may be given a second office action that is not final. The introduction of the Stickle patent caused the examiner not to make his second office action the final action.

In the event of a final office action, provisions of Rules 1.113 and 1.116 under *35 U.S.C. 132* (Code of Federal Regulations: 37) define for you, the applicant, what actions you can take to get further consideration of your application. Rule 1.113, which deals with final rejection on actions, states:

(a) On the second or any subsequent examination or consideration, the rejection or other action may be made final, whereupon applicant's response is limited to appeal in the case of rejection of any claim (Rule 1.191), or to amendment as specified in Rule 1.116. Petition may be taken to the Commissioner in the case of objections or requirements not involved in the rejection of any claim (Rule 1.181). *Response to a final*

TABLE 1-1. General Requirements for Patent Drawings

Symbols, Legends	Graphical drawing symbols and other labeled representations may be used for conventional elements when appropriate, subject to approval by the Office. The elements for which such symbols and labeled representations are used must be adequately identified in the specification. While descriptive matter on drawings is not permitted, suitable legends may be used, or may be required in proper cases, as in diagrammatic views and flow sheets or to show materials or where labeled representations are employed to illustrate conventional elements. Arrows may be required, in proper cases, to show direction of movement. The lettering should be as large as, or larger than, the reference characters.
Views	The drawing must contain as many figures as may be necessary to show the invention; the figures should be consecutively numbered if possible in the order in which they appear. The figures may be plain, elevation, section, or perspective views, and detailed views of portions of elements, on a larger scale if necessary, may also be used. Exploded views, with the separated parts of the same figure embraced by a bracket, to show the relationship or order of assembly of various parts are permissible. When necessary, a view of a large machine or device in its entirety may be broken and extended over several sheets if there is no loss in facility of understanding the view. Where figures on two or more sheets form in effect a single complete figure, the figures on several sheets should be so arranged that the complete figure can be understood by laying the drawing sheets adjacent to one another. The arrangement should be such that no part of any of the figures appearing on the various sheets are concealed and that the complete figure can be understood even though spaces will occur in the complete figure because of the margins on the drawing sheets.
Paper	8 1/2" ×14" white sheets or 8.25 × 11.69" (DIN size A4) Two ply or three-ply bristol-board is preferred. Paper should be erasable even with the use of India ink. The use of white pigment to cover lines is not acceptable.
Ink	India Ink
Instruments	Drafting instruments, which produce clear, sharp, dark lines. Radiograph and even some felt-tip pens can be used.
Character of Lines	Lines should be clean, sharp, solid black with uniform thickness. Every line and letter (signatures included) must be absolutely black. Crowded lines should be avoided. Solid black should be used for sectional surface shading. Free-hand work should be avoided wherever possible.
Margins of Sheets	8.5"× 14" sheets should have a top margin of 2" and margins of 1/4" at the bottom and both sides. Borders are not allowed. For a foreign application (on 8.25" × 11.69" sheets) have a top margin of 1", a right side margin of 0.59", and a bottom margin of .4".
Top of Sheets	The top is always one of the shorter sides of the sheets.

TABLE 1-1. ***(continued)***

Hatching and Shading	(1) Hatching should be made by oblique parallel lines spaced sufficiently apart to enable the lines to be distinguished without difficulty. (2) Heavy lines on the shaded side of objects should preferably be used except where they tend to thicken the work and obscure reference characters. The line should come from the upper left-hand corner at an angle of 45 degrees. Surface delineations should preferably be shown by proper shading, which should be open.
Scale	The scale to which a drawing is made ought to be large enough to show the mechanism without crowding when the drawing is reduced in size to two-thirds in reproduction, and views of the portions of the mechanism on a larger scale should be used when necessary to show details clearly; two or more sheets should be used if one does not give sufficient room to accomplish this end, but the number of sheets should not be more than is necessary.
Reference Characters	The different views should be consecutively numbered figures. Reference numerals (and letters, but numerals are preferred) must be plain, legible, and carefully formed, and not be encircled. They should, if possible, measure at least one-eighth of an inch (3.2 mm) in height so that they may bear reduction to one twenty-fourth of an inch (1.1 mm); and they may be slightly larger when there is sufficient room. They should not be placed in the close and complex parts of the drawing as to interfere with a thorough comprehension of the same, and therefore should rarely cross or mingle with the lines.
Arrangement of Views	All views on the same sheet should stand in the same direction and, if possible, stand so that they can be read with the sheet held in an upright position. If views longer than the width of the sheet are necessary for the clearest illustration of the invention, the sheet may be turned on its side so that the top of the sheet with the appropriate top margin is on the right-hand side. One figure must not be placed upon another or within the outline of another.
Figure for *Official Gazette*	The drawing should, as far as possible, be so planned that one of the views will be suitable for publication in the *Official Gazette* as the illustration of the invention.
Extraneous Matter	Identifying items (such as the attorney's docket number, inventor's name, number of sheets, etc.) not to exceed 2-3/4 inches (7.0 cm) in width may be placed in a centered location between the side edges within three-fourths inch (19.1 mm) of the top edge.
Transmission of Drawings	Drawings transmitted to the office should be sent flat, protected by a sheet of heavy binder's board, or may be rolled for transmission in a suitable mailing tube; but must never be folded. If received creased or mutilated, new drawings will be required.

rejection or action must include cancellation of, or appeal from the rejection of each claim so rejected and, if any claim stands allowed, compliance with any requirement or objection as to form.

(b) In making such final rejection, the examiner shall repeat or state all grounds of rejection then considered applicable to the claims in the case, clearly stating the reasons therefor.

Rule 116 addresses amendments after a final action by the examiner. It states:

(a) After final rejection or action (Rule 1.113) amendments may be made canceling claims or complying with any requirement of form which has been made, and amendments presenting rejected claims in better form for consideration on appeal may be admitted; but the admission of any such amendment or its refusal and proceedings relative thereto, shall not operate to relieve the application from its condition as subject to appeal or to save it from abandonment under Rule 1.135.

(b) If amendments touching the merits of the application be presented after final rejection, or after appeal has been taken, or when such amendment might not otherwise be proper, they may be admitted upon a showing of good and sufficient reasons why they are necessary and were not earlier presented.

(c) No amendment can be made as a matter of right in appealed cases. After decision on appeal, amendments can only be made as provided in Rule 1.198, or to carry into effect a recommendation under Rule 1.196.

After the rejection of my first response, I used up a good bit of my allotted response time trying to determine what recourse I would have if my second amendment to the application were rejected. The examiner, on examining the first response or any subsequent responses, can make the rejection final. If the examiner makes a rejection final, your response is limited to an appeal to the commissioner. In making a final rejection of an application, the examiner will repeat or state all grounds of rejection considered applicable to the claims in the case. In my case, the examiner stated that Claim 2 of my application would be allowed if the *35 U.S. C. 112* was satisfied. After the final action of the examiner, you are limited in your responses to those set forth in Rules 1.113 and 1.116.

Normally, after a final rejection, no other amendments are permitted unless you can show good reason why you did not present them earlier. You cannot, however, respond to a final rejection with matter that causes any new issues, or with matter that amends the claims in a manner other than that suggested by the examiner.

If the examiner indicates that the case will be allowed if you amend the claims in a particular way and you agree with the examiner, you should submit an amendment similar to that discussed in my first response to the examiner (Figure 1-8). But if you disagree with the examiner, you can take one of the following actions:

- *Arrange a phone interview with the examiner.* During the phone conversation you can, in most cases, come to some agreement with the examiner to get the case allowed with amended claims. Figure 1-7 shows my copy of an interview with the examiner of the patent discussed in this chapter after his first rejection.
- *Appeal your case to the Board of Appeal.* To do so, you must file a notice stating that you appeal to the Board of Appeals from the examiner's final action, and submit an appeal fee. The appeal must be filed within 60 days with the brief fee. If you decide to appeal a final action you should study Rules 1.191 and 1.181 of the Title-37 *Patents, Trademarks, and Copyrights.*
- *File a continuation application.* A continuation is a second application for the same invention claimed in a prior application and filed before the original becomes abandoned. The continuation disclosure must be the same as the original application; that is, it should contain no new matter. Then, why does one file a continuation application? The continuation application allows the inventor to introduce into the case *a new set of claims* and to establish a right to further examination by the primary examiner. You can use this technique to establish a first-to-file date—then to write a set of valid and defensible claims in the event of an interference claim. You are probably going to find this dodge above your interest and expertise—for the moment—but it will be a skill to learn in time. Form 8 in Appendix B shows the proper form of the Continuation Petition.

If, after reviewing the examiner's final rejection, you agree with his position and cannot find anything patentable about the invention, you have no choice but to abandon the application. But do not cave in without careful consideration of the merit of your invention.

1.6.1 How to Avoid Caving in Too Early If Your Idea Has Merit

Returning to Figure 1-3, you will notice that the statutory period for my response to the PTO was three months. If you decide that you cannot put together an adequate response to an office action in the allotted time, you can purchase some breathing room. Extensions of the time for a response may be purchased for a fee. The fees for extensions of up to four months are given in Appendix B. Extensions must be obtained before responding to an office action. Failure to respond to an office action within the period of time specified by the examiner will cause the application to become abandoned. However, even in cases where your application is abandoned or circumstances make it impossible for you to frame a proper response to an examiner's rejection within the given time, you still have a chance at getting your patent. Below I discuss ways that you can achieve your goal in spite of a false start.

1.6.2 Petition to Revive

If you fail to reply to an office action in the time allotted by the examiner, the PTO declares your application abandoned. Early in my learning process I had one application declared abandoned because I failed to respond to an office action in a timely manner. I considered this an unintentional abandonment. If abandonment is unintentional, you have the right, under *37 CFR 1.137*, to file a "Petition to Revive" to save the application. If you can show the commissioner to his satisfaction that your failure to prosecute was unintentional or that the delay was unavoidable, your application will be revived.

To do this, you will need to file a "Petition to Revive Due to Unintentional or Unavoidable Abandonment," addressed to the Commissioner of Patents and Trademarks. Form 14 of Appendix A shows a sample petition to revive. This petition should include:

- The title—"Petition to Revive."
- An explanation of why you believe the failure to prosecute was unintentional or unavoidable.
- A statement, in the body of the petition, that: you declare that all statements made therein are true and that you understand that willful, false statements may result in criminal punishment and loss of validity of the application or patents issued thereon.
- Your signature.
- A check; for a small entity (see fee structure in Appendix B).

1.6.3 Continuation-In-Part

After I received my first office action, I realized that the specification of the patent application that I filed could have been stronger. If I had believed in the commercial viability of the manual pusher, I would have filed for a continuation-in-part (CIP).

A CIP is an application filed during the lifetime of an earlier application by the same applicant. The CIP repeats some substantial portion or all of the earlier application and may add matter not disclosed in the earlier case. If it satisfies the requirements of *35 U.S.C. 120*, the CIP application can claim the filing date of the earlier application. The requirements of *35 U.S.C. 120* are that the CIP must:

- Be filed by the same inventor.
- Contain or be amended to contain a specific reference to the earlier filed application.
- Be filed before the patenting or abandonment of, or termination of, proceedings on the first application; or an application similarly entitled to acquire the benefit of the filing date of the first application.

The CIP allows an inventor latitude to change his application to the extent necessary without loss of the filing date of the original application. This latitude is not without cost. You will have to pay fees equivalent to that of a new application.

The need for a CIP can arise under several conditions. For example, you file an application that, in the examiner's view, does not satisfy *U.S.C. 112*. That is, the specification is deficient in a fundamental way, or the specification lacks the identification of a crucial element needed in order for the invention to work. In this case, the CIP, which is filed at a later date, acts to protect your claim to the prior filing date.

1.7 SUMMARY: LESSONS LEARNED IN MY FIRST ENCOUNTER WITH THE U.S. PTO

From my early encounters with the PTO, you can see that:

- Failure to present the application in the form required by the PTO can result in the application's being rejected, even though the idea is patentable.
- The language of the claims must be clear and unambiguous.
- Lack of obvious similarities between one's invention and the prior art (existing patents and publicly known devices or concepts) is not sufficient for a device to be patentable.
- You must do a good search and a thorough review of the patents (prior art) found.
- You must understand the U.S. PTO standards concerning drawings.
- You must be familiar with the patent codes or have access to a copy of the *Manual of Patent Examining Procedure.*

- It costs approximately $800 to $1,000 to prosecute your own patent application.
- The application must consist of a standard set of forms and should meet a standard format (Chapter 5 discusses the format and required forms).

Also, although my first prosecution did not show it, you need to keep records during the course of the invention process.

The remainder of this book discusses record keeping, how to perform a search, what is patentable (patentability), the parts of (construction of) a utility patent, design and plant patent applications, innovation, and infringement and validity.

2

Record Keeping/Protecting Your Idea

Few independent inventors realize the importance of a well-indexed and documented notebook. Many regard the process of systematically recording the chronological developmental history of an idea as a chore. Unfortunately, the task is somewhat bothersome, but you must endure it. Because the granting of patents in the United States is based on which inventor had the idea first (rather than which files first, as in other countries), your "invention diary" could provide you with valuable evidence in your patent pursuit.

You will use your record book to plot the entire course of an idea, from conception through the development of a prototype or working model. Because you cannot know whether an idea is going to lead to a patentable invention, the record book is potentially a valuable legal record. Besides providing legal certainty, the mere act of writing down your observations and thoughts can have a positive effect on your thinking and reduce the chance that you may repeat old mistakes.

Before I describe how to keep notes, I shall give some reasons why you must have a notebook. I have arranged them in order of their importance to the inventing process, which involves conceiving, building, and testing the invention, and then filing a patent application.

2.1 REASONS FOR KEEPING RECORDS

There are three primary reasons for keeping good records:

- For use in the inventing process.
- For use in an interference proceeding.
- For use in a legal controversy.

This section explains each of these reasons in detail.

2.1.1 For Use in the Inventing Process

Good record keeping during the course of a development effort has a salutary effect on your thinking process. Often, it is only when you have tried to summarize your work on a given project that you discover how muddy your thinking is and just what you have to learn to do before proceeding to a successful conclusion of the project.

Many outstanding inventions have not been the result of planned experimental or developmental efforts. Instead, they resulted from observations of unexplained or unanticipated behavior of certain parameters during the course of a developmental effort. Patterns in the behavior of certain parameters become obvious when you can read the record instead of relying on your memory. If you are not in the habit of keeping good records, you may make minor changes in your experimental setups without recording them. Undocumented changes can result in wasted effort and incorrect conclusions.

Let us look at one example where the recording of observations made the difference between sure failure and a success. The invention was an experimental radiation detector for use in the nation's nuclear reactor safety program. I was a member of a group of physicists in this effort, which was trying to develop an incore directional neutron detector. Early in this program, we discovered that the detector did detect neutrons, but it also was sensitive to gamma rays. Try as we might to reduce the gamma ray sensitivity, the daily logs of experimental results revealed that attempts at gamma ray compensation were ineffective. However, the log books also revealed that the device was detecting gamma rays in precisely the same manner that we had hoped to detect neutrons—with direction. Thus, our log books gave rise to the development of a directional gamma ray detector.

We suffered from a "mind set" that resulted in our pursuing a neutron-based detector solution to the problem of designing a directional radiation detector. There in our notes, staring us squarely in the face, was the solution. Fortunately, we recorded all our observations, which revealed that a gamma ray detector would exhibit the directional characteristics required of the detector.

If we had not recorded the results of each experiment and the changes in the design of the detector, the program would have ended on a negative note. We never would have invented an incore radiation detector.

Your notebook also can be a repository for many other ideas. As you work, you frequently will have ideas for new experiments, designs, and concepts. Write them down. If you do not, you may forget them.

2.1.2 For Use in an Interference Proceeding

When two or more patent applications for the same device are filed by different inventors, the patent can be granted to only one of them. Therefore, the PTO starts a proceeding known as an "interference" to determine who is the first inventor and entitled to the patent. About one percent of the applications filed become involved in an interference proceeding. Also, if a patent is issued for an invention that is substantially equivalent to a device for which you have filed an application, you may start an interference proceeding against the patent, provided that:

- The patent was not issued for more than one year before you filed your application.
- Your application is not barred from being patentable for some other reason.

If you are involved in an interference action, you and the owner of the patent must submit evidence establishing when you made the invention. Because the PTO needs to prove various facts and circumstances about the making of the invention, you must be able to produce evidence. If you do not produce something like your well-documented notebook, you run a serious risk of losing an interference action. If you do not submit any evidence, the PTO considers that the invention date is the date you filed.

A board of three interference examiners uses the evidence you have provided to determine which inventor has priority. If the decision of the Board of Patent Interferences goes against you, you may appeal to the Court of Customs and Patent Appeals or file a civil action against the winning party in the appropriate U.S. district court.

2.1.3 For Use in Legal Controversy

If you are making a notebook record that you can use as legal evidence, you need to do primarily what you would do in making a scientific record, but with one important difference: you have to give the subject matter and dates of a notebook entry legal certainty (because they are used in legal proceedings). Thus you need to have someone who understands the subject matter witness each notebook entry. This witness should be someone who not only has read and understood the entry, but has observed and understood the work described and the results obtained. *Contrary to popular belief, a notary public is very seldom a competent witness. A fellow worker or associate is better.* The witness(es) should state in writing that he or she has read and understands the entry in the notebook before affixing his or her signature and the date to the entry.

I cannot overemphasize the importance of properly witnessing a notebook record. If you are not familiar with patent law, you may not realize its importance. Because it is a bother, it is very easy to neglect having your notebook records witnessed. Many reasons have been given for the requirement for an independent corroborating witness in patent cases. One reason is that the interests of the inventor are such that he or she, like an erring politician, cannot be trusted; but the most common explanation for the rule is simply that if the inventor's testimony or records alone were sufficient to establish the date and details of the invention, it would be practically impossible to disprove the evidence in a patent case.

There are court decisions that appear to indicate that an inventor's testimony may be corroborated by the surrounding circumstances, or by records alone, if the court believes that such records could not have been altered. However, where bound records reporting work were introduced into evidence in an attempt to prove that an invention actually had been done, the Court of Customs and Patent Appeals (in Teter v. Kearby, 169 F. 2d 808) stated that it did not think that the facts or the operations recited in the notebooks could properly be held to prove themselves merely by identifying those who made the entries. Simply put, your records should be properly witnessed and dated at each step in the development of your invention.

The general rule in PTO and court proceedings is that the acts of invention must be corroborated by the testimony of an independent witness. Testimony by such an independent witness as to facts that took place several years prior to the testimony ordinarily must be supported by written records, such as notebook records.

In the event that a notebook entry is inscribed by an independent witness, the witness, when called upon to do so in a legal controversy, should identify his or her signature and remarks on the notebook page and further testify that he or she read and understood the entry on the page at the date indicated on the page. The notebook entry and the testimony as to what the witness saw on the page establish only the date of conception of the invention disclosed. Conception alone, however, is not sufficient to establish that an invention was made. There must also be a *reduction to practice*, either *actually*, by making and demonstrating the usefulness of the invention, or *constructively*, by filing a patent application with the U.S. PTO.

In accordance with U.S. patent law, in interference cases, the one who first reduces to practice is regarded as the first inventor unless some other person can show prior conception, coupled with diligence in reducing his invention to practice. Therefore, it is necessary to establish reduction to practice and obtain corroboration of successful use of the invention. No matter how honest you are, your word is never enough to prove you had the invention first. Therefore, be prepared. Have ready the testimony of a person other than yourself who has observed what you have done and the results you obtained in making and testing the composition, article, machine, or process of your invention. This independent witness may be someone who has observed the work of the inventor and the results the inventor obtained.

An independent witness may introduce notebook records to show what he observed and to enable him to fix the date. Such written records may be dated entries made by the independent witness in the form of a dated statement in your record notebook. Such a dated statement should say that the witness observed your work and confirms the results reported in the notebook.

Alternatively, your witness may make an independent dated inscription. This could be in the form of entries in your witness's notebook, describing work he did for you under your direction; for example, to check or confirm your conception or previous work you had done.

2.2 THE CONTENT OF YOUR NOTEBOOK

So that your notebooks have maximum usefulness for establishing legal rights, I offer these recommendations:

- Use a permanently bound notebook. Make the entries in ink, and in chronological order. *Never erase or smudge out an entry.* If it is incorrect, draw a line through it and continue in a fresh space. If the entire page is wrong, do not tear it out; draw a few lines through it and continue on the next page. Never go back and alter or amplify entries made on previous days. Put down the additional data under their own date and cross-reference them to the previous entries. This precaution protects you from any suspicion that you have changed the record or removed something damaging.
- Include the data and an *explanation of the data* in your notebook. Explain the object of the work. Summarize the data, and clarify what they mean. Give the *results* and the *conclusions*. This information is immediately useful to you or your patent attorney/agent in preparing a patent application. You must state objectives, advantages, uses, preferred operating conditions, operable and preferred ranges of conditions, and alternate specific materials and classes of materials. You or your attorney will need all your data, if available. If they are not available, you need to include your opinions about ranges of conditions and alternate substances and procedures. Record ideas, as well as work.
- Sign and date each notebook on the inside front cover.
- Date each page or entry. A single date at the top of each page is sufficient although you can make several entries on the same day. When you make entries for several days on one page, date each entry separately.

- When it is absolutely necessary to use separate loose-leaf sheets or forms, date, number, sign, and have each of these sheets witnessed. Cross-index these sheets with the notebook, and fasten them into it if you can.
- Whenever you think you have a useful invention, such as a new and useful composition, machine, process, or article of manufacture, be sure to make an entry. Then have it read by someone else on or about the date when the entry is recorded. That someone should be a person capable of understanding and describing the invention. Of course, look for someone besides a coinventor, as your coinventor is an interested party, and the courts will discount his or her testimony. Get an independent witness who can legally corroborate your word in a patent controversy. Have this independent witness *sign his or her name* and the *date* at the end of the section of the notebook with a statement that he or she has read the information he or she is witnessing (and identify the information in his or her statement—describing it as a new alloy, new process, etc.) and understands it. Inventors with new ideas often get someone to rubber-stamp entries. In many cases, the person does not understand the invention. This can cause problems if the patent is ever contested in a court of law.

If I seem obsessed about these details, it is for good reason. The patent law protects your hard work, but only if *you* protect *it* by proper documentation. Have a person you trust observe your work and the results you obtain. Have that person state his or her observations in the margins of each page, sign his or her name unfailingly, and give the date on which he or she observed your work and your results. Better yet, have more than one witness. You can lose one witness through death or an uncommunicated move. Two or three witnesses give you more security.

Because it is difficult to know whether or not one's work actually is the groundwork for something patentable, I have found it valuable to have my notebook entries reviewed and witnessed once a week. That way, I have the corroborating witnesses I might need for *all* entries in *every* notebook.

Figure 2-1 is a sample of a fact sheet that I use in my bound notebook. I fill it in at the completion of every project. A fact sheet such as Figure 2-1 will provide you with the information needed to conduct a search.

With your project completed, you are ready to perform a search. However, you could have started the search process as soon as you were convinced that you could reduce your idea to practice. If you work for a large company, there is no real rush to see whether or not the idea is patentable until it has been reduced to practice; but if you are a lone inventor, like me, you cannot afford to work on a device for which you can get only limited protection. In this case, you should perform some kind of search early in the process. The next chapter tells you how to perform either a cursory or a thorough search.

Invention Record No.

1. Name(s) (Full name required).

2. Citizenship.

3. Residence.

4. General nature of the invention:
   (a) Composition of Matter ( )
   (b) Article of Manufacture ( )
   (c) New Compound ( )
   (d) Process or Method ( )
   (e) Apparatus ( )

   Note: If (b) or (c), attach drawing, blueprint, or photocopy showing the invention; if (d) attach flow sheet if capable of illustration.

5. Description of Invention: (Give structure, mode of operation, and results if Apparatus; give details of structure if Article; give steps if Process; give components, proportions, and synthesis if Composition of Matter; give chemical formula, synthesis, melting and/or boiling point if New Compound).

6. Advantages of the invention over what is in use.

7. Earliest conception date: (Give day, month, and year; specify records relied upon).

8. Date of earliest sketch or drawing: (Attach original or photocopy thereof).

9. Earliest disclosure to others: (State where, when, and to whom:)
   Date:
   Name:
   Address:

10. Earliest date of application or reduction to practice: (If practiced, state when, where, and names of witnesses present).

11. Further work is intended along the following lines.

FIGURE 2-1. Sample Fact Sheet

2.3 PTO DISCLOSURE DOCUMENT PROGRAM

The PTO operates a program whereby it will accept invention disclosures and maintain them for a period of two years or more. Under this program the PTO agrees to act as your witness for a fee per invention. The PTO becomes your witness in the event of an interference or other legal situation.

To participate in the disclosure program, all you need to do is to submit a letter, in duplicate, requesting participation. Appendix A shows a sample letter (Form 10). It also shows the form of a Disclosure Document Reference Letter (Form 11), which you should submit to the PTO if you file a patent application related to your original disclosure to the PTO.

2.4 SUMMARY: RECORD KEEPING/PROTECTING YOUR IDEA

In summary, your notebook should show:

- The date you conceived of the invention, the results sought, and how you expect to accomplish them.
- Evidence of diligence on your part in reducing the invention to practice (for example, ordering of parts, assembly of a model, or acts showing continuity of effort).
- Tests, fabrication, manufacturing equipment and test results, pictures, sketches, notes, etc., pertinent to an invention and its reduction to practice.
- Final reduction of the invention to practice, that is, reports of tests of the device, apparatus, or program that demonstrated its operability, or in the case of a process, its feasibility.
- The names of any coinventors.
- Any other notes that might later help your witnesses recall your work, results, and dates involved.

Before I discuss how to search the prior art, let me reiterate the importance of record keeping. Good records and notes are important; do not get caught without them. If your idea is useful and a commercial success, you may have to use your notebook to help you protect your intellectual property. Apart from this obvious reason, an equally important reason for keeping a good notebook is that compiling it will aid you in the innovation process.

3

The Search Process

Your idea is probably not unique. Someone, somewhere, probably has had the same idea. In all probability, a patent exists for it. But you may have an innovative way of doing the same thing, or at least an improvement on the way the original patentee claimed it should be done. So what can you do? If the original patentee has already developed as good a device as yours, it would be pointless for you to pursue the development of your device. Therefore, you will want, as cheaply as possible, to find out whether your device appears in the literature or is patented. To do this, you need to perform a patent search.

There are two basic kinds of patent searches:

- State-of-the-art (i.e., a review of the literature, both technical and nontechnical).
- Patentability (or a novelty search).

The results of these two searches will help you to answer questions concerning validity and infringement when you write your claims.

At the idea stage, you should conduct only the state-of-the-art search. It will tell you whether you should proceed with your invention or start on something new. If you are knowledgeable about new developments in the field of your idea, the state-of-the-art search may be skipped.

Before I describe the stages of a patent search, you must be aware that the search, even if done by a professional, will never be perfect because neither you nor your agent/attorney can search pending patent applications filed before you made your invention.

You get out of the search what you put into it. You can get an excellent job done at a modest cost and without much sweat. Your search effort will vary, depending on the complexity of your invention and how close you are to Washington, D.C., or to one of the public libraries listed in Table 3-1.

These public libraries are Patent Depository Libraries (PDLs), and they receive copies of full patents each week and maintain collections for public consultation. They all have access to the Classification And Search Support Information System (CASSIS), the online database of the PTO, to assist users of patents. If you do not live in one of the cities listed in Table 3-1, you may still be lucky. There are many libraries not listed in the table that have the compact disc version of CASSIS, which gets updated every three months. Check your local public or college library. It may have the CD-ROM version of CASSIS.

If you are a thorough, methodical person, you can, in a day or so, do as good a state-of-the-art or patentability search as you can buy. If you are like me, and choose to perform your own search, you will, after reviewing existing patents, come away from the search with some new ideas.

3.1 HIRE A PROFESSIONAL TO PERFORM THE SEARCH

If you do not want the headaches associated with a search, you can locate attorneys/agents who perform these searches by checking the Yellow Pages of local telephone directories. They will normally be listed under the heading "Patent Searchers" or "Patent Attorneys." You may also review the CASSIS attorney file, or other professional patent publications such as *The Journal of the Patent Office Society*, for searchers. There are also universities with programs where, for a reasonable fee, you can get a search done. In any case, after you identify potential searchers, exercise the same prudence you would observe in any purchase of a service of this importance. Typically, the cost will vary between $300 and $500, the cost for the search being largely a function of the complexity of your invention.

To get a good search done, be sure to provide the searcher with a clear and comprehensible drawing and summary (see Figure 2-1) that describes your invention in a brief and understandable manner. Then list for the searcher the salient features of your invention and any prior art of which you are aware.

Typically, a search performed by a professional will include the art in which the search was conducted and copies of the patents discovered. The attorney also will provide you with an assessment of the patentability of your invention. Figure 3-1 shows an example of the results of a professional search.

Notice that the searcher used the sketches and written information I provided. As I mentioned previously, you should be very careful to provide your patent attorney with a detailed description of what you believe to be the

TABLE 3-1. Patent Depository Libraries with Collections of U.S. Patents

The following libraries, designated as Patent Depository Libraries (PDLs) receive current issues of U.S. Patents and maintain collections of earlier issued patents. The scope of these collections varies from library to library, ranging from patents of only recent years to all or most of the patents issued since 1790.

These patent collections, which are organized in patent number sequence, are available for use by the public free of charge. Each of the PDLs, in addition, offers supplemental reference publications of the U.S. Patent Classification System, including the Manual of Classification, Index to the U.S. Patent Classification, Classification Definitions, and provides technical staff assistance in their use to aid the public in gaining effective access to information contained in patents.

CASSIS (Classification And Search Support Information System), which provides direct, online access to Patent and Trademark Office data, is available at all PDLs. Facilities for making paper copies of patents from either microfilm or paper collections are generally provided for a fee.

Since there are variations in the scope of patent collections among the PDLs and in their hours of service to the public, anyone contemplating use of the patents at a particular library is urged to contact that library, in advance, about its collection and hours in order to avert possible inconvenience.

State	Name of Library	Phone Number
Alabama	Auburn University Libraries	(205) 844-1747
	Birmingham Public Library	(205) 226-3680
Alaska	Anchorage: Z.J. Loussac Public Library	(907) 261-2916
Arizona	Tempe: Noble Library, Arizona State University	(602) 965-7607
Arkansas	Little Rock: Arkansas State Library	(501) 682-2053
California	Los Angeles Public Library	(213) 612-3273
	Sacramento: California State Library	(916) 322-4572
	San Diego Public Library	(619) 236-5813
	Sunnyvale Patent Clearinghouse	(408) 730-7290
Colorado	Denver Public Library	(303) 571-2347
Connecticut	New Haven: Science Park Library	(203) 786-5447
Delaware	Newark: University of Delaware Library	(302) 451-2965
District of Columbia	Washington: Howard University Libraries	(202) 636- 5060
Florida	Fort Lauderdale: Broward County Main Library	(305) 357-7444
	Miami-Dade Public Library	(305) 375-2665
	Orlando: University of Central Florida Libraries	(407) 275-2562
Georgia	Atlanta: Price Gilbert Memorial Library, Georgia Institute of Technology	(404) 894-4508
Idaho	Moscow: University of Idaho Library	(208) 885-6235
Illinois	Chicago Public Library	(312) 269-2865
	Springfield: Illinois State Library	(217) 782-5430
Indiana	Indianapolis-Marion County Public Library	(317) 269-1741
Iowa	Des Moines: State Library of Iowa	(515) 281-4118
Kentucky	Louisville Free Public Library	(502) 561-8617
Louisiana	Baton Rouge: Troy H. Middleton Library, Louisiana State University	(504)388-2570

TABLE 3-1. ***(continued)***

State	Name of Library	Phone Number
Maryland	College Park: Engineering and Physical Sciences Library, University of Maryland	(301) 454-3037
Massachusetts	Amherst: Physical Sciences Library, University of Massachusetts	(413) 545-1370
	Boston Public Library	(617) 536-5400 Ext. 265
Michigan	Ann Arbor: Engineering Transportation Library, University of Michigan	(313) 764-7494
	Detroit Public Library	(313) 833-1450
Minnesota	Minneapolis Public Library and Information Center	(612) 372-6570
Missouri	Kansas City: Linda Hall Library	(816) 363-4600
	St. Louis Public Library	(314) 241-2288 Ext. 376
Montana	Butte: Montana College of Mineral Sciences and Technology Library	(406) 496-4281
Nebraska	Lincoln: Engineering Library, University of Nebraska-Lincoln	(402) 472-3411
Nevada	Reno: University of Nevada-Reno Library	(702) 784-6579
New Hampshire	Durham: University of New Hampshire Library	(603) 862-1777
New Jersey	Newark Public Library	(201) 733-7782
	Piscataway: Library of Science and Medicine, Rutgers University	(201) 932-2895
New Mexico	Albequerque: University of New Mexico General Library	(505) 277-4412
New York	Albany: New York State Library	(518) 473-4636
	Buffalo and Erie County Public Library	(716) 858- 7101
	New York Public Library (The Research Libraries)	(212) 714-8529
North Carolina	Raleigh: D.H. Hill Library, North Carolina State University	(919) 737-3280
Ohio	Cincinnati and Hamilton County, Public Library of	(513) 369-6936
	Cleveland Public Library	(216) 623-2870
	Columbus: Ohio State University Library	(614) 292-6175
	Toledo/Lucas County Public Library	(419) 259-5212
Oklahoma	Stillwater: Oklahoma State University Library	(405) 744-7086
	Salem: Oregon State University	(503) 378-4239
Pennsylvania	Philadelphia, The Free Library of	(215) 686-5331
	Pittsburgh, Carnegie Library of	(412) 622-3138
	University Park: Pattoe Library, Pennsylvania State Library	(814) 865-4861
Rhode Island	Providence Public Library	(401) 455-8027
South Carolina	Charleston: Medical University of South Carolina Library	(803) 792-2371

TABLE 3-1. ***(continued)***

State	Name of Library	Phone Number
Tennessee	Memphis & Shelby County Public Library and Information Center	(901) 725-8876
	Nashville: Stevenson Science Library, Vanderbilt University	(615) 322-2775
Texas	Austin: McKinney Engineering Library, University of Texas at Austin	(512) 471-1610
	College Station: Sterling C. Evans Library, Texas A&M University	(409) 845-2551
	Dallas Public Library	(214) 670-1468
	Houston, The Fondron Library, Rice University	(713) 572-8101 Ext. 2587
Utah	Salt Lake City: Marriott Library, University of Utah	(801) 581-8394
Virginia	Richmond: Virginia Commonwealth University Library	(804) 367-1104
Washington	Seattle: Engineering Library, University of Washington	(206) 543-0740
Wisconsin	Madison: Kurt F. Wendt Library, University of Wisconsin, Madison	(604) 262-6845
	Milwaukee Public Library	(414) 278-3247

unique features of your invention. The quality of your search results will depend to a great degree on what he or she understands about your invention. Also, if you are aware of any devices or inventions that fall within its general area, be sure to make the attorney aware of them. If you decide that you want to perform your search, the following sections detail the steps you must follow.

3.2 STATE-OF-THE-ART SEARCH

To conduct a state-of-the-art search, you must:

- Check trade associations and trade publications in the field of your invention.
- Check the technical journals and product magazines if the invention is of a scientific or an engineering nature.
- Visit stores and product shows in the area of your idea.
- Review the *Reader's Guide to Periodical Literature*, which you can find in your public library, for journals or magazines that service the field of your invention.

You should, with great care, also ask people in the field if they are aware of anything like the invention you are contemplating. In the conceptual stage,

Re: Shooting Toy
Our File #4121

Dear Mr. LeVert:

As requested, we have had a search conducted in the U.S. Patent and Trademark Office directed to your shooting toy. More specifically, the search was directed to shooting toy comprising an infrared emitter designed to turn on a photo-diode sensitive to infrared radiation of a prescribed frequency. The emitter is designed to resemble a gun or other weapon and is provided with a suitable power supply and trigger mechanism, the trigger mechanism being used to initiate the infrared beam and to initiate means for creating sound effects such as the sound of a phaser. The beam from the infrared emitter is columnized such that the beam is suitably narrow. When the photodiode is activated by the infrared beam, a five volt pulse is generated to trigger a musical integrated circuit chip which through the use of a speaker produces the sound of an explosion. The photodiode is further provided with a suitable power source and a sensor concentrator all housed in a target assembly. An electronic filter is provided to filter flickering light and preclude inadvertent activation of the photodiode. The invention was further described in sketches and written information provided us at the time of our initial conference.

The following patents, copies of which are enclosed, were located during the course of the search:

Patent No.	Issue Date	Inventor
3,294,401	December 27, 1966	G. Nichols, et. al.
3,434,226	March 25, 1969	J.W. Schwaller
4,054,290	October 18, 1977	A.J. Villa
4,257,612	March 24, 1981	A.J. Villa

You will note from the patents which were located in the search, the concept of a shooting toy using infrared light is old in the art and not per se patentable. For instance, 4,054,290 discusses a shooting device which emits both infrared and visible light with the target being triggered by the infrared light emissions. Further, patent number 4,257,612 discloses improvements to patent number 4,054,290 with regard to avoiding the inadvertent activation of the target by spurious light or noise harmonics. The others disclose various related devices and concepts.

There is an outside chance that some limited protection may be obtained on certain features of your invention. However, the value of such protection, obtained, is questionable. After you have reviewed the patents enclosed, please contact us to discuss any further advantages over the references.

FIGURE 3-1. Results of a Professional Search

it is unlikely that someone will steal your idea, and sometimes you can avoid reinventing the proverbial wheel.

An instructive example from my own experience shows how you can gain knowledge by talking to people informed in a given field. I had what I thought to be an original idea for a flow meter that worked on the combined principles of a linear voltage differential transformer and a drag disk momentum flux indicator. Following the steps above, I conducted a search of the technical literature. I found no similar device. However, when

I happened to run into a senior instrumentation engineer who sold flow measuring devices, I told him I was thinking of making such a device. I was deliberately vague in my description, of course! The engineer promptly remembered that some 15 years earlier he had seen a device that worked using the same principles, and proceeded to give me the name of the company that held the patent rights to it. I saved myself considerable time and effort because I talked to a person knowledgeable in the field of my invention, and so can you.

Barring this kind of luck, if the results of these tentative actions reveal no device, process, or innovation that anticipated the idea you have, then the next major step is to conduct a patent search. Before you do this, or engage a patent attorney or agent to do it for you, answer the following questions:

- Is there a utilitarian or recreational need for your device or process?
- Can you profitably produce and distribute it?
- Can you, or an agent acting on your behalf, find a licenser (i.e., somebody interested in purchasing the rights to your invention)?

If you answer yes to these questions, it is time for the patentability search.

3.3 THE PATENTABILITY SEARCH

You are lucky if you live in Washington, D.C., or near one of the libraries listed in Table 3-1. If you live near one of these facilities, you can perform your own search. The scientific library of the PTO is a short trip by car, bus, or taxi from downtown Washington, D.C. Located at Crystal Plaza, 2021 Jefferson Davis Highway, Arlington, Virginia, it makes available to the public probably the best scientific library in the United States. It contains more than 120,000 volumes of scientific and technical books in various languages, about 90,000 bound volumes of technical journals, more than 8,000,000 foreign patents in bound volumes, and, of course, all issued U.S. patents, arranged according to classes and subclasses.

In the library's search room, all U.S. patents are divided into more than 300 subject classes and more than 64,000 subclasses. By searching in these classified patents, you can determine, before actually filing an application, whether an invention has been anticipated by a U.S. or foreign patent (i.e., a foreign patent filed in the United States). The search room contains a set of U.S. patents arranged in numerical order and a complete set of the *Official Gazette of the U.S. Patent and Trademark Office* . Patents issued since July 10, 1962 are recorded on microfilm; but those starting from the first one in 1836 up to July 10, 1962, are bound in volumes placed all around the room. Some of the classes and subclasses have been computerized, making a search in these cases almost enjoyable.

If you cannot travel to this search room, you can do an adequate search in one of the PDLs listed in Table 3-1. A small number of these libraries have all the patents that have been issued, from patent number 1 to the present. All, however, will have copies of patents issued since 1962. All have the *Index to the U.S. Patent Classification*, the *Manual of Classification*, the manual of *Patent Classification Definitions*, the *Annual Index of Patents*, the *Official Gazette of the U.S. Patent and Trademark Office*, and copies of issued patents. The addition of the CASSIS system to the PDLs has reduced the time required for a thorough search.

These volumes are the tools needed to perform a search, whether in the search room of the PTO or in a public library:

- The *Index to the U.S. Patent Classification* is an alphabetical list of subject headings referring to specific classes and subclasses of the classification system.
- The *Manual of Classification* contains the various classes and subclasses and relevant subclasses.
- The *Manual of Classification Definitions* defines the class and provides a general list of classes you should search.
- The *Annual Index of Patents* provides an index of patents issued in terms of class and subclass.
- The *Official Gazette of the U.S. Patent and Trademark Office*, a weekly magazine published by the PTO, contains an abstract or claim and a single drawing of each patent issued in that week.

Subclass listings on 16 mm microfilm from research publications are available at many of these libraries. The listings contain the numbers of all patents ever issued, presented by their current assignment of class and subclass.

As I mentioned in Chapter 1, I completed my first search at the Chicago Public Library. Below I reproduce the actual steps I took in my first visit to this library to conduct a search.

3.4 MY FIRST SEARCH OF THE PATENT LITERATURE AT THE CHICAGO PUBLIC LIBRARY

I was somewhat overwhelmed by the activity in the patent section of the Science and Industry Library. People who appeared to know what they were doing were scurrying about and looking very busy. Finally, after checking around and looking busy myself, I went over to the clerk and asked for help. After a quick introduction to the patent section of the Science and Industry Library, I got started. I followed three basic steps:

1. Identify the pertinent class or classes.
2. Identify the pertinent subclasses.
3. Locate pertinent patents.

3.4.1 Identify the Pertinent Class(es)

My first step in the search process was to identify the class of my invention—a manual automobile pusher. To do this, I first consulted the *Index to the U.S. Patent Classification*. The index consists of an alphabetical listing of natural language terms, phrases, synonyms, and acronyms characteristic of products, processes, machines, and compositions of matter that are the subjects of a patent disclosure. Using the index, I located the pertinent field of search—by finding the terms that, to me, best represented my subject matter of interest (i.e., jacks, pushing/pulling implements). If, in following this procedure, you cannot find a match, look for terms with approximately the same meaning.

Table 3-2 reveals the various classes and subclasses I found under the heading "jacks." The class 254 seemed to me to be the most pertinent class for my invention. My invention was traversing (254/84), contained a rack (254/95), and was designed to be attached to a vehicle (254/418). Based on these facts, I searched the class 254. Table 3-3 shows a partial list of the various subclasses of class 254. From the subclasses listed under 254, I identified subclasses 35, 95, 84, and 105 as pertinent to my invention.

In each subclass you will find a first group of patents that belong in that subclass and a second group called cross-references (XRs), which belong to another subclass but are listed there because they have features that make the XR appropriate.

3.4.2 Identify the Pertinent Subclass(es)

My second step was to study the *Manual of Classification* to determine, from among the existing choices identified in the *Index*, the precise classification identity of my subject of interest. By reviewing each major and minor subclass, I identified nearly all relevant subclasses. In cases of subclasses that I was unsure of, I consulted the manual of *Patent Classification Definitions*. By now, I was certain of the class of my invention, and because it was designed to push a vehicle, I looked up the definition of "Pushing and Pulling Implements" under class 254. Figure 3-2 shows the definition.

Under the definition of pushing and pulling implements in the search notes (cross reference), information is provided to guide you to other parts of the classification system that might be helpful. In this case, the manual suggested that I should search Metal Working, Class 29; Tool Driving or Impacting, Class 173; Tools, Class 81, Subclass 3.1 to 3.49; Miscellaneous Hardware,

TABLE 3-2. Example of the Various Classes and Subclasses Listed Under the Jacks

Index to U.S. Patent Classification		
JACKS		
BENDING 3 POINT	72	389
BOOT	223	114+
FLOOR	254	11+
HYDRAULIC	254	93.R
CRANE HOIST CABLE	212	250
CRANE MAST	212	203
MOTOR AND PUMP	60	325+
JACK OR JACK STAND	D34	31
KNITTING NEEDLE	66	123+
DOUBLE END MACHINE	66	63
JACQUARD MACHINE	66	215+
PIPE OR ROD	254	29.R
PUMP	74	41
RACK AND PINION	254	95+
ROLLER FOR CONVEYORS	193	42
SCREW	254	98+
SHOE LAST SUPPORT	12	26+
SMOKE FOR SHEDS	104	52
STEP BY STEP TRAVELING BAR	254	105+
TELEPHONE SWITCHBOARD SPRING TYPE	379	316
THILL COUPLING	254	28.5
TRAVERSING	254	84+
VEHICLE ATTACHED	254	418+
WEIGHING	177	146

Class 16, Subclass 32; and many others. Often, a brief review of the class definition will suffice. However, if after reading the definition you cannot exclude the class, you must check the various subclasses. The definitions, which are updated as the classification system changes, can provide vital links and leads in your search.

The classification system (see Table 3-3) is arranged in a hierarchical manner. The dots preceding a subclass are used to rank subclasses; the more dots, the lower the ranking. Major subheadings under class 254, Implements or Apparatus for Applying Pushing or Pulling Force, are shown in uppercase letters. For example, a major subheading is subclass 35, CAR-PUSHER TYPE. The next major subheading is subclass 39.

Two subclasses under subclass 35 have two dots each—subclasses 38 and 37. These are the most subordinate, as the rest of the subclasses under subclass 35 have only one dot. I chose subclass 38 (two dots), which is ranked beneath subclass 36 (one dot). I chose subclass 38 because I believed it contained patents relative to my invention.

TABLE 3-3. Partial Listing, Class 254: Implements or Apparatus for Applying Pushing/ Pulling Forces

Subclass #	Subclass Title
35	CAR-PUSHER TYPE
36	. Pinch Bar
37	. . Rail clamping
38	. . Pivoted wheel engaging member
39	DOOR BRACE
84	TRAVERSING JACK
85	. Screw
418	VEHICLE ATTACHED JACKS
95	RACK AND PINION
96	. Screw pinion
97	. Geared
98	SCREW
99	. Derrick type
100	. Special engaging feature
101	. . Rocking head or base
102	. Telescoping screws
103	. Geared
104	WEDGE
105	STEP-BY-STEP TRAVELING BAR
106	. Clutch actuated
107	. . Multiple driving clutches
108	. Pawl actuated
109	. . Multiple driving pawls
110	. . . Reversing
111	. . Reversing
112	Rack and lever
113	SINGLE THROW LEVER AND BAR
120	SINGLE THROW LEVER
121	. Rail or tie lifter
122	. Lazy tongs
123	. Lever-supported thrust bar
124	. Mechanically actuated
126	. . Screw
127	. . Cable
128	. . . Block and tackle
129	. Adjustable
130	. . Multiple fulcrums
131	. Special engaging feature
131.5	. . Fulcrumed fork or shovel
132	. . Root puller type
387	LOAD ENGAGING MEMBER AND POWER TRANSMITTING CABLE FOR SHIFTING MEMBER RELATIVE TO STRUCTURE WHICH CONTACTS AND GUIDES MEMBER
133R	SPECIAL ENGAGING ELEMENTS
133A	. Sharing props nonhydraulic

This class includes implements for applying a push or pull directly to an object to be moved or upon which pressure or tension is to be exerted. It comprises jacks (including lifting jacks, floor jacks, stump extractors, and analogous implements), stretchers (including belt, carpet, and wire stretchers), hoisting trucks, and cable hauling apparatus.

With the exception of some patents in cable hauling apparatus, this class does not include the power-applying elements of machines, such as pumps or presses, nor the adjusting elements of articles, such as tables and chairs.

It may, however, include supports of general application not elsewhere classifiable when they comprise means for hoisting the load-carrying portion of the support.

Implements for performing compressing operations upon material--e.g., clamps and bundling devices--are excluded, also devices for merely grasping or engaging with something to be moved, unless regarded as a mere attachment for or element of the pushing or pulling implement.

Pushing or pulling implements of the jack or crow-bar type, including those having special engaging features, which engage between spring elements only will be classified in Class 254. Those implements which engage between a spring and other structure, to move or guide the spring into assembled or disassembled position, will be classified in Class 29, subclasses 700+...

FIGURE 3-2. Class 254, Pushing and Pulling Implements Class Definitions

A further scan of the class revealed a second major subheading, subclass 95. In each of the cases where I believed that a subclass (major subheading such as 35 in Table 3-3) related to my invention, I inspected the schedule starting at that major subheading (e.g., 35).

Major subheadings within a class are always left-justified. All minor subheadings are indented. To search for related patents, start at the lowest-ranking related minor class (i.e., the class with the most dots) and select, in the order of increasing rank (fewer dots), all related minor subclasses above it.

This process resulted in my selecting the class/subclasses 254/35, 36, and 38. Likewise, I selected 254/105, 108, 111; 254/120, 124, 126; and 254/133R to search for related patents. In all cases, you should start at the major subheading related to your invention, select the first appropriate second line (one dot) subclass, proceed to the third line (two dots) items, and find the most appropriate subject heading. Continue this process until a higher ranking (fewer dots) subheading intervenes, or you encounter a major subheading within the class.

Major subheading 105 provides a more interesting case than 35 (see Table 3-3). Because my invention did not contain a clutch, I skipped 106 and its inferior subclass 107, selecting instead 108. My device was not covered by 109, so I skipped it also, leaving 111. Thus, in this case, I selected the major subheading 105 and minor subclasses 108 and 111 under class 254 to search for patents.

The classifications are frequently expanded. The need for expansion is indicated by an R appended to a subclass number (e.g., 133 R in Table 3-3). The "alpha" category shown in 133 A is the result of an informal expansion of the examiners. The *Manual* contains different listings. In the preliminary pages there are lists in which patent classes are arranged by related subjects, or an alphabetic approach to the classes using the words in the titles. You may wish to use these listings to make your entry to the class schedule instead of the approach I used. Personally, I believe these lists are better left to more experienced searchers. Once you make your way to the *Manual* to search subclasses, be aware that the subclass numbers are not in numeric order. You may find, as in the 254 class, subclass 88 (not shown in Table 3-3) preceded by subclass 300. Therefore, you must scan the entire class.

Finally, with hindsight, it may be instructive to see what class and subclasses the PTO examiner searched in his examination of my Manual Automobile Pusher application. According to the "Field of Search" topic in the patent (see Appendix E), they were 254/1, *35, 95-97, 108—111, 120, 124, 126,* 129—130, 131, *133.* I identified all of these during my search, but chose to search only those italicized, plus subclass 105. The correlation between the class and subclasses I selected and those selected by the examiner was very good. This agreement supports the assertion that you can do a first "class" search.

3.4.3 Locate Pertinent Patents

Having satisfied myself that I had identified the appropriate classes and subclasses, I was ready to move onto the *U.S. Patent Classification—Subclass Listing* in search of the classes and subclasses identified in my second step. The subclass listing lists patents in ascending order, starting with the oldest patent.

Table 3-4 illustrates a fraction of the total 121 patents found under class 254, subclass 35. There were some 198 patents listed for subclass 95. Starting with a list of 121 patents in subclass 35 and an equal or greater number in the other subclasses was overwhelming. Where was I to begin? Some of the patent numbers were followed by an X, meaning that they were cross-reference

TABLE 3-4. Selected Number of Patents From U.S. Patent Classification Manual for Class 254 Subclass 35

1328770 O	1342761 U	1416755 O	1483116 O	1641398 O	1803583 U	1850065 X
1886588 X	1891795 X	1913792 X	1938658 U	2014351 X	2053080 X	2060526 O
2134440 X	2391657 U	2473109 O	2621892 O	2623476 X	2639888 O	2642221 O
2723104 U	2760755 O	2948508 O	3029065 O	3099435 O	3567299 X	3614115 X
3653330 X	3770136 O	3793964 X	3826198 X	3826199 X	3826200 X	3826201 X
3828690 X						

assignments. Original assignments (i.e., patent numbers followed by a zero) by the examiner are determined by the most comprehensive claim allowed by the examiner. All other claims are assigned to cross-reference categories.

To aid you in your search, each volume of the *Index to the U.S. Patent Classification* contains a table for the year, entitled "List of Patent, Design, Plant Patent, Reissue and Defensive Publications Numbers Appearing in the Individual Issues of the Official Gazette." The *Gazette* contains the name of the invention, a major claim or an abstract, and one figure of each patent issued during the given year. For example, Table 3-5 provides the issue date, volume and number of the *Gazette* patent types, for patents from number 4,131,952 through 4,179,752 issued in 1979. You can use the *Gazette* to determine whether you want to acquire the full patent for further study. Because the patents in the PDL libraries are not separated by classifications, finding them can be time-consuming.

Once you have obtained a copy of a pertinent patent, you should read it carefully, paying particular attention to classes and subclasses listed under the title "Fields Searched." Often, you will find classes and subclasses that you did not consider in your search. Bear in mind that although a patent may not be in the field or class of your invention, it is possible that it could be combined with one or more issued patents in your field to make your invention unpatentable.

If you want to search the foreign prior art, take a look at Volume 9 of the *International Patent Classification* entitled *Guide, Survey of Classes, and Summary of Main Groups,* for detailed procedures for searching the international patent system.

TABLE 3-5. List of Patent, Design, Plant Patent, Reissue and Defensive Publication Numbers Appearing in the Individual Issues of the Official Gazette for 1979

			First Number in Issue				
Issue of	Vol.	No.	Patents	Designs	Plant Patents	Reissues	Defensive Publications
Jan. 2	978	1	4,131,952	250,676	4,360	29,872	T978,001
Jan. 9	978	2	4,133,052	250,736	None	29,877	None
Jan. 16	978	3	4,134,152	250,796	4,363	29,879	None
Jan. 23	978	4	4,135,252	250,856	4,369	29,887	None
Jan. 30	978	5	4,136,402	250,916	4,371	29,889	None
Feb. 6	979	1	4,137,572	250,976	4,373	29,897	T979,001
Feb. 13	979	2	4,138,742	251,036	4,377	29,904	None
Feb. 20	979	3	4,139,912	251,096	4,381	29,913	None
Feb. 27	979	4	4,141,082	251,156	4,385	29,919	None

TABLE 3-5. ***(continued)***

			First Number in Issue				
Issue of	Vol.	No.	Patents	Designs	Plant Patents	Reissues	Defensive Publications
Mar. 6	980	1	4,142,252	251,216	4,390	29,923	T980,001
Mar. 13	980	2	4,143,422	251,276	4,394	29,928	None
Mar. 20	980	3	4,144,592	251,336	4,396	29,936	None
Mar. 27	980	4	4,145,762	251,396	4,400	29,944	None
.	.	.	.	.	.	.	.
.	.	.	.	.	.	.	.
.	.	.	.	.	.	.	.
June 5	983	1	4,156,942	251,996	4,423	30,017	T983,001
June 12	983	2	4,157,592	252,056	4,424	30,025	None
June 19	983	3	4,158,242	252,116	None	30,033	none
June 26	983	4	4,158,892	252,176	4,429	30,038	None
July 3	984	1	4,159,542	252,236	None	30,040	T984,001
July 10	984	2	4,160,292	252,296	4,432	30,042	None
July 17	984	3	4,161,042	252,356	4,437	30,043	None
July 24	984	4	4,161,792	252,416	4,441	30,049	None
July 31	984	5	4,162,542	252,476	4,444	30,056	None
Aug. 7	985	1	4,163,292	252,536	4,445	30,062	T985,001
Aug. 14	985	2	4,164,042	252,596	4,448	30,070	None
Aug. 21	985	3	4,167,792	252,656	4,451	30,075	None
Aug. 28	985	4	4,168,542	252,716	4,455	30,083	None
Sept. 4	986	1	4,166,292	252,776	4,458	30,088	T986,001
Sept. 11	986	2	4,167,042	252,836	4,459	30,092	None
Sept. 18	986	3	4,167,792	252,896	4,460	30,096	None
Sept. 25	986	4	4,168,542	252,956	4,461	30,100	None
Oct. 2	987	1	4,169,292	253,016	4,462	30,104	T987,001
Oct. 9	987	2	4,170,042	253,076	4,463	30,108	None
Oct. 16	987	3	4,170,792	253,136	4,464	30,112	None
Oct. 23	987	4	4,171,542	253,196	4,465	30,120	None
Oct. 31	987	5	4,172,292	253,256	4,470	30,127	None
Nov. 6	988	1	4,173,042	253,316	4,475	30,135	T988,001
Nov. 13	988	2	4,173,792	253,376	4,480	30,143	None
Nov. 20	988	3	4,174,542	253,436	4,485	30,151	None
Nov. 27	988	4	4,175,292	253,496	4,490	30,159	None
Dec. 4	989	1	4,176,407	253,556	None	None	T989,001
Dec. 11	989	2	4,177,522	253,616	None	30,162	None
Dec. 18	989	3	4,178,637	253,676	None	30,167	None
Dec. 25	989	4	4,179,752	253,736	None	30,175	None
Last No. for 1979			4,180,806	253,795	4,490	30,182	T989,005

At the time when I performed my first search in the Chicago Public Library, the Classification And Search Support Information System (CASSIS), the online database of the Patent Office, was not available at PDLs. In addition to now being available at all PDLs, it also has been introduced as a CD-ROM product by the U.S. PTO, and is in use at libraries other than those listed in Table 3-1. The online system available at PDLs includes access to the *Index to the U.S. Patent Classification*, the *Manual of Classification*, *Patent Classification Definitions*, three years of abstracts as a word pool, and the *Manual of Patent Examining Procedure* (MPEP).

You will not use the MPEP in your search. It can be very useful in helping you to fashion your response to an office action, however. It contains instructions to examiners (as well as other material about interpretation) and outlines the current procedures that the examiners are required or authorized to follow in the normal examination of a patent application.

A search using a CD-ROM version of the CASSIS system at the University of Tennessee with the manual pusher as the subject is discussed below. The CD-ROM version of CASSIS provides the same information as the online version. The most recently released patent information of the CD-ROM version lags the online version by three months. The CD-ROM version is found in many non-PDL libraries throughout the United States.

3.5 SEARCHING: USING CASSIS

A search using the menu-driven CASSIS system can save you a great deal of time. CASSIS provides you with the searchable files shown in Figure 3-3. As in the case of the manual search, if you are lacking any knowledge about existing inventions, you can start by selecting the *Index to the U.S. Patent Classification* from the CASSIS search mask. CASSIS allows you to input terms for searching such as the one shown in Figure 3-4, and provides you with a tally of the number of related topics appearing in the index. The system allows you to browse related topics. Notice that in Figure 3-4, I left the classification query blank. The system returned a long list of related topics—with corresponding classes and subclasses. From this list, you may select the "appropriate" class or classes.

With hindsight, I selected class 254, and proceeded to the CASSIS bibliographic files, selecting class 254 and the class title: Implements or Apparatus for Applying Pushing or Pulling Force. The result was a listing of all subclasses, numbers, and titles under 254. The subclasses are not arranged in numeric order, so I had to scan the entire list, just as I did with the manual search. Likewise, CASSIS provides the class definition (see Figure 3-3),

Reassignment File
Attorney Roster File
USPC to IPC Concordance
Classification Order Index
Classification Definitions
Index to the U.S. Patent Classification
Patentee - Assignee File
Manual of Patent Examining Procedure - PAGE
Manual of Patent Examining Procedure - TITLE
Manual of Classification File - PAGE
Manual of Classification File - TITLE
Bibliographic/Assignee File
Classification Info. File - by Subclass
Classification Info. File - by Patent No.

FIGURE 3-3. CASSIS Searchable Files

complete with search notes. As before, the class definition serves to support or question the choice of the search class, and provides hints of other classes that need consideration in your search.

Satisfied with the choice of class, one must move on to the classification files, which are arranged by subclass and patent number. Once a class/subclass combination is provided, CASSIS, when the page mode is selected, will give a printout of all patents issued for that class/subclass, starting at the most recently assigned number in the database (a list identical to that of Figure 3-4 except in reverse order). If the title mode is selected, the CASSIS system will provide a printout of that portion of the classification system represented by the search results. That is, the hierarchical structure related to a certain major subclass is clarified. The title mode presentation for the class/subclass 254/35 is given in Figure 3-5 with all of the nonrelated minor subclasses under 105 excluded.

In the example given above, I performed a subject search to determine the class/subclasses relevant to my invention. I could have determined the appropriate class/subclasses in several different ways. These different approaches are given in Figure 3-6.

Search Index

Index to the U.S. Patent Classification

Index Term: pushing and pulling implements
Classification:

FIGURE 3-4. Terms Supplied as Input to CASSIS to Obtain Alphabetical Listing of Related Classes and Subclasses

```
Clsf Selected: 254/105

1. 254 PUSHING OR PULLING IMPLEMENTS
2. 254/105 STEP-BY-STEP TRAVELING BAR
3. 254/108 'Pawl activated
4. 254/111 ''Reversing
```

FIGURE 3-5. CASSIS Search Title Mode Output for Class 256 and Subclass 105

If you know the (assignee) name of a company making the product, a patent number (which appears on objects, etc.), or the title of the invention or the inventor, you can use these facts to start a search in the patentee assignee file of CASSIS. Or if you have a patent number, then a patent number search in the classification information file, by file number, will provide you with a class and subclass number as a starting point for stepping directly into the *Manual of Classification* files to look for other subclasses, and so on.

If you are not sure that you have searched the correct class/subclass, you can, using a patent search request similar to that shown in Appendix A (Form 12), ask the staff at the Public Search Room in Arlington, Virginia, to suggest the proper class/subclass numbers for your search. Also, CASSIS provides an attorney roster file that you can use to look for a source of professional help, if you need it.

In addition to CASSIS, there are other online databases that you may use to do your search at a library. The PDL nearest your home can provide you with information about these online services.

a. Use Index to US Patent Classification and enter words or terms; relevant class/subclass numbers can be reviewed and selected.

b. Use Manual of Classification-Title and enter classification title words.

c. Use Classification Info File by Patent No. and enter relevant known patent number(s) to review assigned class/subclass.

d. Use Manual of Classification-Page and browse class/subclass, if you have has a general idea of class number.

e. Use Bibliographic/Assignee and enter terms from title/abstract; look at resulting patent class numbers to identify relevant ones.

(The number of patents assigned to a specific class/subclass, search Classification Info File by Patent Number; enter class/subclass and total number of patents will be indicated.)

FIGURE 3-6. CASSIS: Subject Searching for Class/Subclass Identification

3.6 MY FIRST SEARCH AT THE PTO

By the time I conducted my first search at the PTO, I was a seasoned veteran. I went prepared with my log book and a list of key words that described my invention. Once inside the PTO, you can perform your search in the public search room or in the examining division. The difference between the two locations is that, in the examining division, the search (I think) goes faster. You can get help (by asking for it) from the examiner who performs searches in your class.

Besides having the help of an expert, you will find that having the patents separated by class, and, more important, subclasses, in both the public search room and the examiner's search room, will ease your search. Other than the quality of the search I performed, which I attributed to my greater preparedness and my understanding of the process, the two searches were similar. The steps in the search were the same, except that when I identified my subclasses in the public search room, I found them on the shelves. In the examiner's search room, I found them in what are called "shoes." Like the Chicago Public Library, the search room at the PTO has facilities for making copies, or you can purchase coupons from the PTO's cashier, which you deposit in boxes in the search room. These coupons allow you to purchase complete patents. The PTO will mail you the patents within three to four weeks.

3.7 RESULTS OF THE SEARCH: WHAT TO LOOK FOR IN THE DISCOVERED PRIOR ART

There are two main criteria to use to compare your invention to any prior art that you might find. These criteria are:

- Novelty (newness)
- Nonobviousness

This section explains each of these criteria in detail, and gives examples, so you can gain a reasonable understanding of these terms.

3.7.1 Novelty

After you have studied the patents identified during your search, there are several questions you must ask yourself. Is your invention similar in its operation or features to the patents discovered during your search? Do the patents found reveal devices that operate in the same way to achieve the same results? Are the differences between your invention and the prior art insignificant? A negative answer to any or all of these questions is not sufficient to prove the patentability of your invention, nor is an affirmative answer sufficient to render your idea unpatentable. Doublespeak aside, what you can be sure of is that your invention may be the subject of a patent application if it is different in any large or minor way. Further, if it uses a similar machine or process to achieve a different result, it may be patentable. However, even if you answer the above questions in a way that does not cause you to fold your tent, you might always be dogged by difficult questions, such as these: How novel does a new invention have to be? When is an advance an invention and not a minor improvement or an obvious extension of existing inventions?

Let us return to the patent of Chapter 1. When the examiner compared my application with the prior art, he indicated that various patents, by Anell, Nixon, Buddingh, Templeton, and Bryant, together comprise all the features of my invention. None of these patents was a "dead ringer" for mine, but each, according to the examiner, exhibited one or more of the features common to my application. (Appendix E presents several of these patents.)

Further, the examiner stated that the patent of Fotheringham described the various means of my first claim or their equivalents. Fotheringham had one claim that explicitly cited elements for lifting and transmitting force to an automobile.

The examiner believed that Fotheringham's patent revealed a device that operates in a similar manner to mine to achieve similar results, and that anyone skilled in the art of automobile jacks could have made my invention after reviewing that patent.

When you examine the device of my invention, in view of the examiner's comments, the newness or novelty criterion for patentability becomes a difficult thing to measure or to quantify. Regarding the newness standard, Justice William O. Douglas declared that "patents serve a higher end—the advancement of science." The manual automobile pusher clearly fails this test, which is known as the "flash of genius" standard.

Therefore, even though your idea may not meet this standard, you should review all of the discovered art with at least one thought in mind: can you, by studying the prior art, take the elements found therein and develop your device? If you can, then you cannot hope to get patent protection for your idea. However, if you added some new wrinkle that results in a new effect, you have a patentable invention. You may not have satisfied the condition of novelty (newness), but you will, no doubt, meet the more modern standard of nonobviousness.

3.7.2 Nonobviousness

Until 1952, the "flash of genius" standard for newness was applied by most courts to determine whether an invention was patentable. The Patent Act of

1952 changed all of this by substituting a new standard: nonobviousness. This standard declares that an invention would be unpatentable "if the differences between the subject matter as a whole would have been obvious at the time the invention was made to a person having ordinary skill in the art (PHOSITA) to which said subject matter pertains." 'Ordinary skill in the art' includes the educational level of the inventor and other people in the field, the problem solved relative to problems normally encountered in the field, and the sophistication of the field. Obviousness then turns, in part, on what constitutes the ordinary level of skill in an art. For example, does simultaneous invention by more than one individual make an invention obvious? The U.S. Supreme Court has instructed the Patent Office to decide such matters by:

- Examining the prior art.
- Examining the difference between the prior art and the claims of the patent at issue.
- Determining the level of ordinary skill in the art.

The third item is the most difficult one. Through continuing improvements in the definition of what constitutes a PHOSITA, the courts have attempted to help examiners resolve the third item.

To examine how you measure up against the nonobviousness criterion, you must determine whether the prior art describes elements that, though modified by you, retain their essential features or functions. In the patent of Chapter 1, the examiner indicated that the high-friction element of my invention is obvious in view of the friction element of the patent of Stickle (see Appendix E). The examiner is simply saying that my design and function of the high-friction element could easily be derived by looking at the invention of Stickle. Moreover, the examiner said that, when one viewed the inventions of Nixon and Buddingh, elements of each invention can be found in mine.

The examiner, in the case of Stickle, made an important point—because Stickle had claimed the friction element as a part of his invention, I could not claim a modified friction element as an element in my invention. However, if my design for the friction element had produced some unusual, useful effect, then it would have been possible to claim it as an element in my invention.

This example is simple and straightforward, but in many cases what is meant by obviousness is not so clear. Obviousness means that even though your invention is not identically disclosed in previous patents, if the differences between yours and the prior art are such that your invention would have been obvious to a person having ordinary skill in the field of your invention, it is not patentable. It would fail the test of obviousness. Both novelty and obviousness are difficult issues to resolve and are best left to patent lawyers and the courts.

The question I ask myself is this: does the invention produce new and unusual results? If it does, then there is a good chance that a patent will be awarded. The patent our group received for the directional self-powered gamma ray detector (SPGD) discussed in Section 2.1.1 is a good example of an unusual effect achieved using the prior art. Self-powered detectors of gamma rays in the core of a nuclear reactor were well known when we conceived the idea that a certain arrangement of the electrodes in the sensor region of the detector could produce a directional effect. Therefore, unlike the existing SPGD detectors, which were sensitive to gammas incident upon them from all directions, this new detector responded primarily to gamma rays incident from one direction. The physics of the devices were the same, but the components had been arranged in such a way as to achieve this result, which was not obvious in view of the prior inventions by PHOSITAs.

3.8 Summary

After the search is completed, whether by you or by a professional searcher, it's time for you to read and try to understand the patents. It is at this point that you wrestle with questions of novelty and obviousness. These are large questions, and I think that, like me, you would want to have certain minimal tools before tackling them. Chapter 4 purports to provide you with those tools. It presents the patent codes that you will have to deal with and provides my view of what they mean in practical language.

4

Your Idea: Is It Patentable?

President George Washington signed the first U.S. patent bill on April 10, 1790. This was a monumental step in the annals of innovations because it recognized, by law, the intrinsic right of the inventor to profit from his invention. Many think that this right of the inventor to profit from his or her labor has been the primary driving force behind much of the progress and the technological advances of the last 100 years.

The patent law has undergone some fundamental changes since its inception, with significant changes in the law occurring in 1793 and again in 1836. The Patent Act of 1836 reestablished the "examination" system, which had been in effect prior to 1793. It reaffirmed the requirement that patentability should be viewed in terms of "prior art."

The patent statutes of 1793 and 1836 embodied Thomas Jefferson's philosophy that "ingenuity should receive liberal encouragement."

4.1 PATENT CODES FREQUENTLY ENCOUNTERED BY THE INDEPENDENT INVENTOR

Whether you decide to prosecute your own patent application or engage an attorney to do it for you, you can expect to have your application rejected in the first office action. Though each case will be different, you can be sure that early in your first encounter with the PTO, the "core" patent codes— *35 U.S.C. 101*, *102*, *103*, and *112*—will be cited by the examiner in your case before you are done with the prosecution. (See the examiner's response in Section 1.3.) Your first encounter with an examiner's action can be an unnerving experience, particularly if the examiner cites U.S. codes with which you are not familiar. To avert this chilling effect, this chapter reviews *35 U.S.C. 100*, *102*, *103*, and *112*, and some others.

The main conditions preceding the grant of a patent to an applicant are set forth in *35 U.S.C. 100*, *101*, *102*, and *103*. These codes cover patentability, lack of novelty (obviousness), and the specifications.

4.2 UTILITY AND PATENT CODES

The principal reason for making a search is to determine whether your invention is patentable. To make a decision as to the patentability of your invention, you must understand the rules of the game.

4.2.1 What is a Patentable Invention?

According to *35 U.S.C. 101*, a patent shall be awarded in response to a patent application that meets the following criterion:

> Whoever invents or discovers a new and useful process, machine, or composition of matter, or any new and useful improvement thereof, may obtain a patent therefor, subject to the conditions and requirements of this title.

What is meant by "this title" can probably best be explained by discussing each of these categories.

- *Manufacture*: The production of articles for use from new materials prepared by giving to those materials new forms, qualities, properties, or combinations, whether by hand labor or by machinery. Two extremes of manufacture are dolls and microorganisms. In between those two, we find the myriad of things we use daily.
- *Machines*: Devices or apparatuses for performing a task. A machine usually does some kind of work and normally has some moving parts. The pusher of Chapter 1 is a machine, and so are automobiles, computers, electronic concepts, telephones, coffee makers, and so on.
- *Processes*: Any technique or method of doing or making things or substances. A process may have one or more steps. Processes are numerous. For example, ways of making chemicals, liquid fuels, drinking substances, certain materials or types of materials, nuclear energy products, and so forth, are all processes.
- *Compositions of matter*: Aggregates, conglomerates, chemical compositions or substances that are usually applied in bulk in gaseous, liquid, or solid states. Examples include concrete, composite building materials, paper, synthetic fabrics, and so on.

A new use of an invention developed and patented under one of the categories listed above is patentable. For example, if you use a dehumidifier to heat water, you have a specific new use for the device and therefore can get a patent for it, even though it has already been patented with a different use.

What cannot be patented? The laws of nature, physical phenomena, abstract ideas, and computer algorithms cannot be patented. Thus, neither a new mineral discovered in the earth nor a new plant found in the wild is patentable subject matter. Likewise, Einstein could not patent his celebrated law ($E = MC^2$), nor could Newton have patented the law of gravity. The patentability of new life forms is presently being argued.

There is a way around the fact that computer programs are not patentable. If you can claim the algorithm as a machine or as a method that uses a machine, then it is possible to effectively patent an algorithm. Just cite hardware in the claim, and avoid the use of the words "program" and "algorithm."

Your invention must also be useful, not a nuclear weapon, and not illegal. It can, however, be considered immoral in some sections of our society. Note also that it cannot be a perpetual motion machine, unless you are prepared to demonstrate it for the PTO! Operability is a requirement for all perpetual motion machines. The meaning of the term "useful process" given in the title is probably best left to legal experts. I am almost certain that anything you invent will be a useful process or device and not illegal.

Today, because of the public concern about the effects of the nuclear revolution, there is a special restriction of nuclear-related inventions. These restrictions mean that you cannot obtain a utility patent for inventions that are useful solely with special nuclear materials (e.g., uranium 235, plutonium 239, and thorium 233) or atomic energy for atomic weapons.

4.2.2 Lack of Novelty or Anticipation

We have discussed what is patentable. Now let us talk about the buts—the conditions that could prevent your getting a patent. This subject is covered by *35 U.S.C. 102*, which defines the conditions for patentability, novelty, and loss of right to patent. According to 35 *U.S.C. 102*, a person is entitled to a patent unless:

1. The invention was known or used by others in this country, or patented or described in a printed publication in this or a foreign country, before the invention thereof by the applicant for patent, or
2. The invention was patented or described in a printed publication in this or a

foreign country or in public use or on sale in this country, more than one year prior to the date of the application for patent in the United States, or
3. He has abandoned the invention, or
4. The invention was first patented or caused to be patented, or was the subject of an inventor's certificate, by the applicant or his legal representatives or assigns in a foreign country prior to the date of the application for the patent in this country or an application for patent or inventor's certificate filed more than twelve years before the filing of the application in the United States, or
5. The invention was described in a patent granted or an application for patent by another filed in the United States before the invention thereof by the application for patent, or
6. He did not himself invent the subject matter sought to be patented, or
7. Before the applicant's invention thereof the invention was made in this country by another who had not abandoned, suppressed, or concealed it. In determining priority of invention there shall be considered not only the respective dates of conception and reduction to practice of invention, but also the reasonable diligence of one who was first to conceive and last to reduce to practice, from a time prior to conception by the other.

That is a real mouthful, but it is understandable. However, items 2 and 7 deserve some further discussion. Item 2 means that if you described your device in a magazine, newspaper, professional journal, printed thesis, or any medium where the description can be assessed by the public one year before you filed your application, you cannot patent it. Also, if you offer it for sale one year before you file your application, you void its novelty. Clearly, to avoid problems, you should always file your application before you offer your invention for sale or publish anything about it.

The patent (U.S. 3,120,606) on a general-purpose computer issued to Eckert and Mauchly for the ENIAC was invalidated because the patent application was determined to have been filed more than one year after public use or sale. The computer was found to have been constructed, fully tested, and successfully operated in December 1945. It was sold to the U.S. Army Ordinance Department before June 26, 1946, a year prior to the June 26, 1947 filing date for the patent application.

Item 7 is somewhat different from the others in that it is judgmental. I like the phrase "diligence of one who was first to conceive and last to reduce to practice." It speaks to the fact that not only must you be able to document that you conceived an idea first, but you must be able to show that you worked (by a documented log book—see Chapter 2) reasonably to reduce it to practice. Consider an example where an inventor observes that using a new detector developed by him in a monitoring system made by Company A would make the system work more efficiently. He records his observation in his log book but does nothing else. Several years pass, and Company A also realizes that the detector can be used with great benefits in its system, without being aware of the inventor or his notebook. Company A applies for a patent, which is awarded. Does the inventor have any legal recourse? No! He cannot show diligence in his effort to reduce his invention to practice.

However, if he had persevered and, because of the lack of resources, failed to beat Company A to the patent with an application, he would have legal recourse. If his log book showed an effort by him to reduce his idea to practice, he would have legal rights to the invention. This hypothetical case points out the importance of maintaining a good, well-documented log book as discussed in Chapter 2, and the importance of carry-through.

4.2.3 Patentability

The conditions for patentability are set aside in *35 U.S.C. 103*: "Conditions for patentability; non-obvious subject matter." According to *35 U.S.C. 103*:

> A patent may not be obtained though the invention is not identically disclosed or described as set forth in *35 U.S.C. 102*, if the differences between the subject matter sought to be patented and the *prior art* are such that the subject matter as a whole would have been obvious at the time the invention was made to a person having ordinary skill in the art to which said subject matter pertains. Patentability shall not be determined by the manner in which the invention was made.

35 U.S.C. 103 simply means that even though your invention satisfies the requirements of *35 U.S.C. 102* in that there are no inventions identical to yours, it may still be unpatentable because existing patents and knowledge would make it obvious to anyone of ordinary skill in the art (Mr. or Ms. PersonHavingOrdinarySkillInTheArt—PHOSITA).

The term prior art, which is the most important part of *35 U.S.C. 103*, means the state of knowledge existing or available before your invention. It is what your invention must differ from in order to be patentable. Prior art is defined by items 2, 4, 5, and 7 of Section 4.2.2; that is, it comprises publications by you or others, public knowledge, existing patents, and general public use. All of these except public use are pretty clear. Some examples of public use are:

- A metal-working technique that achieves a certain desired result that has been passed between machinists.
- A special source for marinating cooked meat that is well-known to certain regional practitioners of the art of cooking.
- A process of firing green porcelain that has been taught to members of a hobby class.

Public use of experimental and developmental purposes cannot be used to deny you a patent as long as the experimental or developmental use was for purposes of testing the device for your evaluation and not to test suitability for the user's purpose.

The use need not be public, however, to be of the type of use that can invalidate your patent. For example, if your invention is a process and you use it to manufacture a product for sale more than a year before filing your application, *35 U.S.C. 102* (Section 4.2.2) bans it by such use from receiving a patent.

To avoid problems, you should bring to the attention of the patent examiner any publication or other prior art that is relevant. The same is true for public use or sale.

4.2.4 Specifications

The invention must be disclosed in a manner acceptable to the PTO. The requirements are given in *35 U.S.C. 112*. According to *35 U.S.C. 112*:

> The specification shall contain a written description of the invention, and of the manner and process of making and using it, in such full, clear, concise, and exact terms as to enable any person skilled in the art to which it pertains, or with which it is most nearly connected, to make and use the same, and shall set forth the best mode contemplated by the inventor of carrying out his invention.
> The specification shall conclude with one or more claims particularly pointing out and distinctly claiming the subject matter which the applicant regards as his invention. A claim or claims may be written in independent or dependent form, and if in dependent form, it shall be construed to include all the limitations of the claim incorporated by reference in the independent claim.

This means that you should write your application in clear and simple language. Do not fall into the trap of trying to write as a lawyer would. The claim or claims may all be independent, or the claims may consist of one independent and several dependent claims. The claim may consist of what are called elements.

4.3 DESIGN AND PLANT PATENT CODES

The United States Codes discussed above are applicable to utility patents. Those codes specifically written for design and plant patents are explained below:

> *35 U.S.C. 171*
> Patents for designs. Whoever invents an original and ornamental design for an article of manufacture may obtain a patent therefor, subject to the conditions and requirements of this title.

A design patent, according to *35 U.S.C. 171*, can be obtained by "whoever invents any new, original, and ornamental design for an article of manufacture." Here "design" means the visual characteristics or aspects displayed by the object, the appearance presented by the object that generates an impression in the eye of the observer. In this context a design may be the shape or configuration, or it may be the surface ornamentation of an object; or it may be both.

A design is inseparable from the object and cannot exist alone merely as a scheme of surface ornamentation. It must be a definite, preconceived thing, capable of reproduction, and not merely the chance result of a method. The design patent protects only the appearance of an article, not its structure or utilitarian features. For example, a lamp shade may be the subject of a design patent, and so can a cabinet of a television set, the shape of a radio, a specially designed chair, and so on. A utility patent and a design patent may be based on the same subject matter, provided there is a patentable distinction between them. The mechanical device shown in Figure 4-1 could be the subject of both a utility and a design patent application. However, I doubt that it could clear the objection of being obvious.

35 U.S.C. 161
Patents for plants. Whoever invents and discovers and asexually reproduces any distinct and new variety of plant including cultivated spores, mutants, hybrids

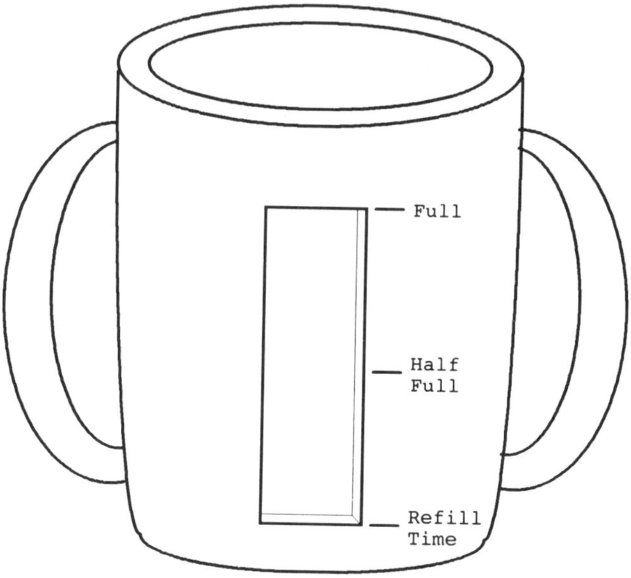

FIGURE 4-1. Drinking Cup

and newly found seedlings, other than tuber propagated plants or a plant found in an uncultivated state, may obtain a patent therefor, subject to the conditions and requirements of this title.

Asexually propagated plants are plants produced by means other than seeds; that is, by use of cuttings, layering, budding, grafting, inarching, and so forth. The term tuber means a rounded form that bears axillary buds. It applies to among other things, Irish potatoes and the Jerusalem artichoke.

Scientists consider bacteria "plants," but they are not included in this act's use of the word.

The details of the application for a plant patent differ from those of other applications. Chapter 6 discusses these differences.

4.4 PROTECTION PROVIDED BY A PATENT

The "protection" establishes authorship of the invention and protects the reputation of the inventor. The ownership of a patent protects the inventor as long as he or she is ahead of other inventors. The protection provided for each type of patent is given in Table 4-1. A patent, however, exposes the inventor's ideas for all to see, and this exposure can lead to circumvention by others. Once most ideas are explained (as in a patent), they become obvious. That means others can, if they desire to do so, evade your claims. On the other hand, if you hold back some vital information, someone may attack your patent's validity.

What the patent really protects is the investment of money and effort that led to the making of the invention, for, if nothing else, your patent puts you at an advantage over your rivals. The measure of the protection, however, is the extent to which you are able to employ your patent either to contain competition or to bargain with your competition.

Table 4-1 lists kinds of protection that patents offer against others using

TABLE 4-1. Types of Patents, Period, and Kinds of Protection

Type	Period of Protection	Extent of Protection Afforded
Utility patent	17 years	Covers articles of manufacture, compositions of matter, apparatuses, and processes.
Plant patent	17 years	Covers new varieties of flowers, trees, fruits or other plants (excluding tubers) created by asexual reproduction.
Design patent	3-½, 7, or 14 years, at option of inventor	Covers novel ornamental appearance of anything that commercially depends on aesthetic appeal.
Structure patent	17 years	Covers structure of an object.
Materials patent	17 years	Covers chemical formulations.

your hard work to enrich themselves. To avail yourself of such protection, you must discover the infringer; and once you do discover the infringer, you have the right to sue to recover damages for past infringement. You can also secure an injunction that prevents the infringer from making, using, or selling anything embodying your invention. The statute of limitations on patent infringement is six years, which means that you can recover damages retroactively for up to six years before the date when you file suit. However, if you are aware of an infringement, you must act rapidly. Otherwise, an infringer can claim that he believed that you would not sue under your patent and thereby can block your suit.

Before you sue, procure all evidence available, such as manuals, photographs, samples of the device, product catalogs, and so on. After gathering this information, you should turn it over to your lawyer, who may choose to request that the infringer pay you royalties for the past usage of your invention and offer him a license under your patent for future activity.

An infringement case must be brought into federal court where the infringer has a place of business and has made, used, or sold the patented invention; so you should select an attorney whose office is in one of these locations. Sometimes it is wise to sue a retailer or purchaser of the invention, as well as the manufacturer, in order to get jurisdiction that is favorable and/or geographically near to you.

Patent infringement suits can be expensive. If you discover an infringer, it may be to your advantage *not* to sue, but to seek some kind of settlement. Also, you can file suit yourself against infringers, without an attorney. The process is very involved. If you choose to proceed on your own, I suggest that you read the book *Patent Litigation: Procedures and Tactics*, by R. S. White, before you act.

The patent process encourages the inventor to make the invention. If it were not for patent law, many inventors would be unable to develop their inventions and would abandon their ideas instead of going forward with them. Many others would keep their ideas secret as long as they could, instead of publishing them in patents, which stimulate others to make further inventions.

This patent protection extends only throughout the territory of the United States and has no effect in a foreign country. A person desiring a patent in a particular country must make an application for patent in that country in accordance with the requirements of that country. Treaties and foreign patents will be discussed in greater depth in Chapter 6.

4.5 OTHER PROPRIETARY ASSETS

The terms proprietary assets, proprietary rights, industrial property, and intellectual property are all names for the same thing. They include, in addition to patents, trademarks, trade secrets and know-how, trade names, and copyrights.

4.5.1 Trademarks

A trademark relates to any word, name, symbol, or device that is used in trade with goods to indicate the origin of the goods and to distinguish them from the goods of others. It is like a brand name. For example, Miller's is a well-known trademark for a brand of beer, and Craftsman is an equally well-known trademark for tools. A trademark does not prevent others from making the same goods or from selling those goods under a mark that is not confusing. Trademark rights that are used in interstate or foreign commerce may be registered in the PTO. Once your trademark is registered, it becomes easier to sue infringers. To register your trademark, write the Commissioner of Patents and Trademarks for the appropriate form.

The trademark should always be used as an adjective with at least its first letter capitalized. Other identifiers may be the use of a diminutive "TM" after it, or preferably, if it is registered, by putting a superscript "R" after it. The principal thing to guard against is the consistent use of a trademark as a noun. This practice can result in the trademark becoming generic and thus usable by anyone who uses the trademark as an adjective modifier. A number of words that were at one time trademarks (aspirin, for example) have become the generic names for products. Another example is the name "monopoly." It has become a generic name and hence can be used by anyone wishing to cash in on its public acceptance and implied meaning.

States require that a device must be used in intrastate commerce before you may register it. To ensure that you have met this requirement, write your state's secretary of state and request the form.

Note that if you have a unique trademark, it is entitled to common law protection. This means simply that you can sue anyone who uses a similar mark. The filing fee for a trademark application, per class, is $200.

4.5.2 Copyright

Though somewhat removed from the general purpose of this book, copyrights are discussed because they are a major proprietary asset. A copyright, simply put, prevents someone from copying something. That something may be literary, dramatic, musical, or artistic. It speaks to the form of expression rather than the subject matter of the writing. You could copyright the description of a machine or an electrical circuit, but that offers protection only against others copying the description. It would not prevent others from writing their own description and making the machine or building the electrical circuit. The only requirement for them is that the method of expression and the particular details are different.

Copyrights, unlike trademarks, are registered in the Copyright Office in the Library of Congress and not in the PTO. The copyright act that went into effect in 1978 may also protect some of the trade secrets of manufacturers. In an Alabama federal court case, a judge stated that the copyright law was designed to establish an exclusive method for determining authorship and ownership and preempts suits for misappropriation of trade secrets that previously could be brought under state laws. Therefore, documents relating to a trade secret must be copyrighted to protect it. However, because a copyrighted document is in the public domain, the court's decision poses a tricky problem for companies seeking to preserve a trade secret.

As with trademarks, common law copyright protection exists provided that a work is published with a copyright notice. This notice may consist of the word "copyright" or the symbol "C," together with the name of the author or whoever owns the copyright, and including the words "all rights reserved." But it is always wise to register the copyright, and unlike patents, there is no time limit on when you must register. To secure the forms for copyrighting a creation, you should write to the Copyright Office, Washington, D.C. 20559. The mechanics of securing copyrights are so simple that many authors and artists secure their own copyright protection.

Table 4-2 summarizes intellectual property, excluding patents, and the rights related to its ownership.

To write a patent application to protect your idea, you must understand the various components of a patent. In the next two chapters, we will study in detail utility and plant and design patent applications, with emphasis on the utility patent application.

TABLE 4.2. Intellectual Property

Proprietary Properties	Protects	Criteria for Grant	Who Grants Rights	Duration of Rights
Trademark	Words, Symbols, etc. used to distinguish goods or services	Not descriptive, distinctive use	Common Law, States, U.S. Government	As long as used, varies 20 +
Copyright	Music, Writings, Recordings, Works of Art, and Labels	Original	Automatic; formalized by application to U.S. Copyright Office	Life of Author plus 50 years; 75 or 100 years for work for hire
Trade Secret	Know-how, Techniques, Mfg. Processes, Customer Lists	Keep secret; Not known to public	Common Law	As long as secret

5

The Utility Patent Application: Guidelines for Drafting a Model Utility Patent Application

Now that you have completed your prior art search and have given some thought to the ease of manufacturing and selling your invention, you are ready either to abandon your idea or to proceed full steam ahead. If you are proceeding, it is time to file the application by yourself or to employ an attorney or patent agent who will file for you. I recommend that you apply for the patent yourself if you think the invention has little commercial potential. This will provide the necessary learning experience to make you more proficient in the art of patent preparation. I am not suggesting that you use the PTO as a learning tool, but rather that you allow the PTO to perform its constitutionally authorized duty.

This chapter details the required layout and content for patent applications. Hopefully, this will keep the application form from slowing you down in getting your patents.

5.1 ARRANGEMENT AND CONTENTS OF THE SPECIFICATIONS

The application you submit to the PTO should contain the following items:

a. Transmittal letter (Form 1 in Appendix A)
b. Certificate of Mailing letter (Form 7 in Appendix A)

c. Drawing(s) on bristol board (See Appendix E)
d. Specifications containing the following sections:
    - Title of the Invention
    - Cross-references to Related Applications (if any)
    - Field of the Invention
    - Background of the Invention
    - Summary of the Invention
    - Brief Description of the Drawing
    - Description of the Preferred Embodiment(s)
    - Description of the Invention
        - — Mode of Operation of Invention
        - — Broadening Statement
e. Claim(s)
f. Abstract of the Disclosure
g. Oath or Declaration form(Form 13 in Appendix A)
h. Small Entity Declaration (Form 16 in Appendix A)
i. Prior Art Statement (Form 9 in Appendix A)

The order of the components of the specification should be arranged in the application as presented above. The specification, claims, and abstract of the disclosure should be typewritten to form one document. The claims and abstract may start new pages. They should be identified as "Claims" and "Abstract." The complete package should be mailed to Commissioner of Patents and Trademarks, Washington, D.C. 20231.

5.1.1 Title of the Invention

Place the invention title at the top of the first page of the specifications. Try to limit the title to seven words or less. If you need more than seven words to provide a technically accurate and descriptive title, use them. For example, suppose you have developed a dual beam ultrasonic flow meter for which you are filing a patent application. You might decide to entitle the invention: "A Dual Beam Ultrasonic Flow Meter for Measuring Fluid Flow in Conveyances." Although this title is technically correct and descriptive, you could condense it to "Fluid Flow Measurement System." The choice of a title is clearly a matter of preference. My experience has shown that the examiners in the patent office seldom object to inventors' titles for their inventions.

5.1.2 Cross-References to Related Application

You should cite all relevant foreign and domestic patents (i.e., prior art) in the field of your invention. When you cite a reference, give the invention's patent number, the inventor's name, and the date of allowance. You may also include class and subclass numbers. If you have based the invention on scientific developments not commonly known, you may also refer to the technical literature (i.e., prior art) in the exact form that follows:

References Cited
United States Patent Documents

3,402,606 9/1968 Bruba............73[1]–194[2]

Other References

H. F. Messios, "Ultrasonics Measures Flow Velocity of Rivers," *Electronics*, Oct. 13, 1961, pp. 56–59.

In addition to referencing the prior art in your application, you should include a separate form about each prior art reference with your original submittal to the PTO (see Form 9, Appendix A). If you send the Statement of Prior Art form in *with your original application*, you need only include the names of the inventors and title of the invention at the top of the form.

You will not know the name of the examiner, the Group Art Unit, and Serial No. when you submit the application.

Following the first paragraph of the form, list all references of which you are aware; for example: "Patent 3,402,606 issued to Bruba, 9/1968: shows an ultrasonic flow measuring device." You may state the difference between the reference and your invention. You must list all references, after which you should close with an expression of respect, your name(s) and your address(es).

You may file a Statement of Prior Art up to 3 months *after* your initial application filing date if you discover additional relevant patents or technical references. Whether you submit it at the time of your initial transmittal or later, you should include a self-addressed, stamped postcard with the following statement:

Application of________________,
Serial No.__________, Filed ______________
Title____.
Received for Filing (to be supplied by PTO).

5.1.3 Technical Field

The technical field statement describes the field of the invention. For a thermal neutron detector it might read as follows: "The present invention relates generally to the detection of thermal neutrons, and more particularly

[1]Denotes class of invention
[2]Denotes subclass of invention

to a solid state detector for thermal neutrons in strong gamma ray fields, as well as to a detector system for use in nuclear reactors and other nuclear systems to accomplish neutron detection therein."

5.2 Background of the Invention

The background of the invention should be a narrative description of the field of the invention and a description of the prior art. Each of these may be written under the general heading of "Background of the Invention" or under subheadings as indicated in Section 5.1. For the hypothetical flow meter, the field of the invention would be flow measurements and could be stated as follows: "This invention relates to fluid flow measurements, particularly to a system for accurately computing volumetric flow rates and related values of a fluid, using ultrasonic measuring techniques." The description of the prior art could be: "Volumetric flow rates in closed conveyances are measured by different techniques, one of which is the Venturi meter, which measures the pressure differential within the conveyances. Use of the Venturi meter requires a long run of straight pipe so that fluid flow is fully developed, a situation that is not always encountered in practice. Further, another method for closed conveyances or open channels includes the introduction of some identifiable material into the flow and measurement of the time required for the material to traverse a known distance. The determination of the correct time interval is difficult, and the sensing head normally obstructs the flow." Note that in each case I have presented the prior art with its deficiencies (real or perceived).

Finally, state the object of the invention. The object of this hypothetical invention might be stated as follows: "It is the object of this invention to provide a system that computes volumetric flow rates accurately and without the objections attendant to prior art types of measurements." As indicated in this statement, you may refer to the general state of the art and to the advance made with your invention, but you are not permitted to make derogatory remarks about the inventions of others. You may not make disparaging remarks about the products or processes of any particular person other than yourself. Nor may you make statements as to the merits or validity of the patents of other inventors. However, mere comparisons with prior art are not considered to be disparaging per se.

5.3 Summary of the Invention

Each application submitted to the PTO needs a summary, the purpose of which is to let interested people know the nature of the invention. You should direct it toward the claims of the invention and not state it in generalities that might apply equally well to many other patents. The summary should describe the exact nature, operation, and purpose of the invention and provide material assistance in aiding a ready understanding of the patent in future searches. Stereotyped general statements, which may be equally well applied to any case, should be avoided. For the hypothetical flow meter, a broad general statement might be: "Volumetric flow rate across a reference plane in closed conveyances is derived by an apparatus that obtains values indicative of the resident time of the flowing medium in the vicinity of the sensor." This statement could apply equally well to a Venturi, an orifice system, a turbine, and other flow meters. Instead, the general statement could be: "Volumetric flow rate across a reference plane of a fluid flowing in a conveyance is derived by an apparatus that obtains values indicative of the differences in the transit times of two simultaneously transmitted ultrasonic beams." This statement is concise and refers only to the hypothetical ultrasonic flow meter.

5.4 BRIEF DESCRIPTION OF THE DRAWINGS

Describe your drawings briefly—the view presented and the name of your invention. You can introduce the drawings with a preamble, or without, as shown in the descriptions below:

- *With preamble*: "The function and advantage of this invention will become more apparent from the following description taken in connection with the accompanying drawings in which:

  Figure 1 is an elevation view, or cross section, of a typical nuclear reactor vessel and vessel internals, also incorporating this invention."

- *Without preamble*: "Figure 1 is a sectional side view of an apparatus for the practice of the present invention."

You must describe each figure in the patent. See the examples in Appendix E.

5.5 DESCRIPTION OF THE PREFERRED EMBODIMENTS

The preferred embodiments include:

- Description of the invention.
- Operation of the invention.
- Broadening statement.

This section describes each of these in detail.

5.5.1 Description of the Invention

You will probably have to refer to your drawings when describing the invention. When you do, use the numbered parts. I use a technique for describing my applications previously referred to as the "bare bones technique." This technique requires that you describe the relations between all the components, starting from a terminal part, verbally constructing the device. If you are seeking a process patent, then start with the base material or solution and proceed to describe the process.

Most likely the application is for an improvement patent. Thus, the description must point out the part(s) of the process, machine, manufacture, or composition of matter that is improved. The description should be confined to the specific improvement—to the necessary parts that cooperate with the improvement and those parts germane to a complete understanding or description of it.

You must be careful to describe all the invention's features on which you will base your claims. Be sure to describe each part of the drawings and its relationship to other components; that is, describe the electrical or mechanical connection of all components. All the information and details in the claims must be included in the detailed description or revealed in the description of the figures. (See examiner's first response to my application of Chapter 1, Section 1.3.) Claims that embody information or details not evident in the figures or the Description of the Invention are always rejected as being new matter. In the course of the description, you should cite alternative designs of components, if applicable, materials, ways of mixing chemical components, and steps that achieve the same end results—if they are to be cited in the claims. If your invention includes more than one embodiment, you must describe each embodiment in the specification.

5.5.2 Operation of the Invention

Finally, the inventor should describe the operation of the invention, again using the numbered parts of the enclosed drawing(s). This wrap-up provides the applicant with the opportunity to identify the uniqueness and function of the elements of the invention.

5.5.3 Broadening Statement

The broadening statement, which follows the discussion of the operation of the invention, broadens the scope of the invention. An example of a broadening paragraph could be as follows: "From the foregoing, it will be apparent to a person skilled in the art that a neutron detector has been developed that will detect neutrons. Although only a limited number of specific embodiments have been described in detail, such description is not to be taken as a limitation of the present invention. Rather, the scope of the invention is to be defined by the appended claims and their equivalents." The broadening statement should be the closing statement of the description of the invention.

5.6 CLAIMS: THE OPERATIVE PART OF THE INVENTION

The claims are the subject matter that you regard as your invention. They must conform to the invention described in the specifications. Therefore, the terms and phrases used in the claims must find clear support or antecedent basis in the description such that the meaning of the terms in the claims may be ascertained by reference to the description. Novelty and patentability are judged by the claim(s), should you market your invention. Questions of infringement and validity will also be decided on the basis of the claim(s) filed. Thus, the need for careful construction of the claims cannot be overemphasized. You may present more than one claim, provided that they are different and not unduly extended in numbers by insignificant variations. Dependent claims are formed by referring back to another claim or claims in the same application. In referring back to a claim, remember that you are further limiting the claim by referring to another claim. Thus, if the independent claim is rejected, the dependent claim also fails.

If your invention is an improvement of an existing patent, the claim(s) should contain:

- A preamble comprising a general description of all the elements or steps of the claimed combination that are common.
- A phrase such as "wherein the improvement comprises."
- After that phrase an indication of those elements, steps, and/or relationships that constitute the portion of the claim that you consider to be new or improved.
- Arabic numerals to number your claims if you have several.
- Your dependent claims grouped together with the claim(s) to which they refer.

Consider the simple examples of claims for different kinds of inventions given below.

Process or Method Claim: Neutron Emission Sensing

A method of monitoring elongated fuel elements, which emits neutrons, of a nuclear reactor core comprising:

providing an elongated instrument element and locating said instrument element in its monitoring position, parallel to said elongated fuel elements;
passing a cooling fluid adjacent to said elongated instrument element;
partially isolating a zone of said instrument element from said cooling fluid such that said zone rises in temperature as a result of neutron bombardment therein;
providing a zone whose temperature depends on the temperature of said cooling fluid; and
measuring the temperature difference between said zones which is directly related to the neutron emissions from said fuel elements.

This claim contains a title and preamble that states the purpose of the method. The claim contains five steps, which state how one would measure the neutron emissions from fuel elements in a nuclear reactor's core.

Apparatus: Fluid Detector

A junctionless thermocouple cable consisting of two thermoelectric elements enclosed in a metallic sheath wherein a negative resistance temperature coefficient insulant is interpositioned between the thermoelectric elements and the inner surface of the metallic sheath thereby providing electrical insulation and thermal energy transfer between the thermoelectric elements;

a metallic sheathed resistance heater, which is used to input thermal energy to the fluid level detector;
an outer metallic cylindrical tube capable of being sealed on one end, into which said junctionless thermocouple cable and resistance heater are inserted and held in place by mechanically swaging or drawing, to reduce the outer diameter of said metallic cylindrical tube, thereby causing mechanical interference and thermal energy transfer between the inner surface of the outer metallic sheath, and the sheaths of said thermocouple cable and said resistance heater; and
separate means for supplying electric currents to said thermoelectric elements and to said resistance heater; and
electronic and computing means for measuring the loop resistance of the thermoelectric elements with a temporary junction, caused by a temperature gradient at an axial location, across an interface between a liquid and a gas in a tank, along said thermocouple cable contained in said metallic cylindrical tube, which is formed when the resistance heater is used to raise the temperature of the level measuring device above the temperature of the liquid in which it is submerged, and for estimating the distance to the temporary junction, and hence the level of fluid using the output of said resistance measuring means.

This claim, like the previous claim, contains a preamble, but it is somewhat more complex in that it contains five elements. The elements are (1) a junctionless thermocouple cable, (2) a sheathed resistance heater, (3) an outer metallic cyclindrical tube, (4) means for supplying power to the heater and the thermoelectric elements in the thermocouple cable, and (5) an electronic and computing means. The claim contains two broad means elements that do not restrict the invention to specific ways of performing certain required functions.

New-Use Claim: Brandy to Grow Hair

A method of stimulating the growth of hair on the heads of middle-aged men comprising frequently washing the heads of such men with brandy to stimulate the growth of hair.

This claim recites a new use for brandy and the purpose of the new use in a manner that avoids the known, old use of brandy.

Composition of matter claims, like all of these examples, must include a preamble and a body containing a recitation of the elements of the composition.

As the claims are the heart of your invention, you should be very careful when writing them. You must avoid numerous mistakes and pitfalls.

Vagueness and Indefiniteness. This means imprecise and unclear wording. In claim one of my first application, I described a "means for providing structural strength to . . . ", without identifying the element that provides the structural strength or how it was connected to other elements of the invention. The claim was rejected as being vague—"not clear"— by the examiner. The examiner must make sure that the wording of the claims is sufficiently definite to reasonably determine the scope. For example, a claim is indefinite if it recites "said rod" and there was no earlier reference or no antecedent in the claim to a rod. An indirect limitation affords a grounds of rejection as indefinite. If a "rod" is set forth and, later in the claim, "said steel rod" is recited, the claim is indefinite.

Incompleteness. The claim is incomplete if it omits essential elements, steps, or a necessary structural cooperative relationship of elements needed to describe an invention.

Prolixity. The claim is prolix when it contains recitations of unimportant details that hide or obscure the invention.

Nonstatutoriness. The claim is not statutory if it fails to particularly point out and distinctly claim an invention. An example is an omnibus claim such as "A device substantially as shown and described."

Aggregation. Here the mistake is that the claim does not establish cooperation between the elements of the claim. For example, an aggregation would be the association of a washing machine with a dial telephone. A rejection on this basis points more to the invention than the claim. A claim is not necessarily aggregative because the various elements do not function simultaneously.

Old Combination. Here a claim is directed to a well-known combination, such as a carburetor claim in combination with a gasoline engine. Because the carburetor has a separate status, it can stand alone in a claim.

Lack of Support in Drawing. The drawings must show every feature recited in a claim. See, for example, the first office action to my automobile pusher, where Claim 3 was rejected because the "worm gear rack post" was not illustrated in the drawing.

Multiplicity. There may be too many claims; that is, an unreasonable number in view of the nature and scope of the invention.

Functionality. A claim or an element may be rejected that contains functional language not supported by recitation of sufficient structure to warrant the presence of the functional language. A claim that recites only a simple means and thus encompasses all possible means for performing a desired function falls into this category.

Correspondence of Claim with Disclosure. The terms or words of the claims must be present in the specifications. If subject matter capable of illustration is claimed, it must be shown in the drawing.

These are not all of the mistakes you can make in trying to frame your invention in the claims. They include those that I have made. If you need additional information on the subject consult the *Manual of Patent Examining Procedure*, available from the Patent and Trademark Office.

Finally, I would like to suggest that you think of the claims of your patent as a fence surrounding the intellectual property you wish to protect. Try to build the fence using broad planks (elements) that prevent easy circumvention. Remember that elements (planks) that can be omitted without loss of specificity concerning what you are claiming as your invention should be excluded.

5.6.1 Numbering of Claims

The original numbers you assign to the claims you submit to the PTO must be maintained throughout all the office actions. If, in the course of your prosecution, a claim is canceled, the remaining claims cannot be renumbered. If you add claims to your existing claims during the prosecution, they must be numbered consecutively starting with the highest numbered claim. In a single-claim patent the claim is not numbered.

5.6.2 Required Punctuation and Form of Claims

It is accepted practice to begin each claim with either "I (or we) claim." Begin each claim with a capital letter and end with a period. Do not use periods within a claim, except for abbreviations. The common form of punctuation is the semicolon. The elements of the claim can be rewritten in paragraph form, with each followed by a semicolon. Always state your claims in decreasing order, from the broadest to which you believe you are entitled to the most detailed. Several of the patents shown in Appendix E are written in this manner. Broadest to narrowest—this should always be the form of your claims.

Typically, the most detailed claims are the dependent claims. That is, the dependent claim normally tells how and with what a function will be accomplished. The dependent claims include all the limitations of the claims to which they refer. You may present one or more claims in dependent form, meaning that they refer back to and further limit a claim or claims in the application.

A claim is accepted as dependent if it refers to another claim. However, it must include every limitation of the claim upon which it depends. In other words, it shall not be infringeable by any device that would not also infringe the basic claim. Thus, if Claim 1 recites the combination of elements a, b, c, and d, a claim reciting the structure of Claim 1 in which d was omitted and replaced by e would not be a proper dependent claim, though it placed further limitations on the remaining elements or added still other elements. The claim with the element d would be an independent claim.

5.6.3 Types of Claims and Filing Fee Calculation

You are allowed a total of twenty claims—three independent and seventeen dependent claims for the basic filing fee of $345, if you qualify as a small entity. You pay this fee even if you have only one claim. This fee was correct as of December 16, 1991. My first application cost $150 to file in 1979. A detailed list of fees is given in Appendix B.

You qualify as a small entity if you are an independent inventor.

5.6.4 Writing the Claims: Things to Consider

The claim aspect of the patent process is critical. An inventor must proceed cautiously if he is to establish claim domination. By claim domination, I mean that the principal claim must contain every aspect of the invention it dominates. If there are facets of the invention that are not covered in the main claim, it may be easy to circumvent the patent. In Chapter 4, in my discussion of infringement, I referred to circumvention as the act of clearing the elements of an existing patent. Several patent disclosures are presented in

Appendix E. The patents exhibited there were chosen because of the simplicity of the claims and because they exemplify the way a good set of claims should be written.

When you construct claims to your patents, you should:

- Examine your invention in view of prior art to determine exactly what is patentable so that you avoid obvious rejection by the examiner.
- Construct the main claims so that all components, processes, or chemical constituents are covered.
- Restrict the claims to those aspects of the invention that can be patented.
- Construct the claim or claims so that the physical or structural characteristics of the components and the relationship between them are clearly delineated. Be careful to show the cooperative connection between the various features or components of the invention.
- Use, where possible, creative repetition in claims such as modifying successive dependent claims to cover specific features of your invention.
- Avoid all discussion of design and color unless they are germane to the operation or functional characteristics of your invention.

5.7 ABSTRACT OF THE DISCLOSURE

The Abstract of the Disclosure should be a concise statement of the technical disclosure of your patent. Include the new aspects of the art that pertain to your invention. If the patent is basic, the entire technical disclosure may be new in the art. However, if the patent is an improvement of a patented apparatus, process, product, or composition, the abstract should discuss the technical disclosure of the improvement. In some cases, particularly those involving compounds and compositions where the process for production or use is not obvious, the abstract should set forth a process for producing or using the compounds and/or compositions.

The following list provides examples of what the abstract should reveal:

In the case of	*You should reveal*
A machine or apparatus	the detail of its operation and organization
An article	the method of making it
A chemical compound	its identity and use
A mixture	its ingredients
A process	the steps involved, exclusive of mechanical design details

Limit the abstract to fewer than 250 words and do not use phrases that can be implied, such as "The disclosure defined by the invention," and so forth.

Also, avoid the form and legal phraseology often used in patent claims, such as "means" and "said." Describe the disclosure in a manner that helps the reader decide whether to consult the full patent text.

Samples of machine/apparatus, process, and chemical abstracts are given below.

Apparatus A directional detector of changes in a local electrostatic field comprising two parallel flat coils of copper wire, separated by an electrically grounded plane rectangular conductor that is coated on both sides with an insulator and associated signal conditioning electronics, has been constructed. The combination of coils and plane rectangular conductors forms two independent wide band antennae which, when placed in an unobstructed electromagnetic radiation field, have induced in them electric currents of equal peak-to-peak values. When the combination was brought near an ungrounded body, such as a person standing on an insulator to earth, a coupling of high frequency potentials of the ungrounded body and the nearest coil occurred, while the coil farthest away from the body (due to the presence of the electrically grounded plane rectangular conductor) remained unaffected. The coupling of high frequency potentials caused an increase in the amplitude of the electric current in the affected coil, which is used in conjunction with the electric current in the unaffected coil and the signal conditioning electronics to actuate an alarm unit.

Process A method for closing, whereby heat is applied to seal overlapping closure panels of a folding box made from paperboard having an extremely thin coating of moisture-proofing thermoplastic material on opposite surfaces. Heated air is directed at the surfaces to be bonded, the temperatures of the air at the point of impact on the surfaces being above the char point of the board. The heat application is so brief (because the boxes are moving so swiftly through the air stream), that the coating on the reverse side of the panels remains substantially non-tacky. The bond is formed immediately after heating. The required bonding time for any one surface point is less than that point's total time of exposure to heated air. Under such conditions, the heat applied to soften the thermoplastic coating is dissipated after completion of the bond by absorption into the board, which acts as a heat sink and eliminates the need for cooling devices.

Chemical Somides are produced by reacting an ester of a carboxylic acid with a somine, using as a catalyst an alkoxide of an alkali metal. The ester is first heated to at least 70°C under a pressure of no more than 450 mm of mercury to remove moisture and acid gases which would prevent the reaction, and then converted to a somide, without heating, to initiate the reaction.

An abstract is not required for a design patent because a design patent is just that—a patent for a design.

5.8 FRAUD: YOU, YOUR APPLICATION, AND THE PATENT OFFICE

There are three types of fraud you need to be aware of:

- Failure to disclose known relevant prior art.
- Failure to disclose technology already in the public domain.
- Misrepresentation of test data to the examiner.

This section discusses each type in detail.

5.8.1 Failure to Disclose Known Relevant Prior Art

The courts have consistently ruled that patent applicants, inventors, and their attorneys are held to the highest standard of moral and ethical conduct. Because a patent gives you, the inventor, a monopoly with respect to the public over the subject matter of the patent, you are expected to conduct yourself in dealing with the PTO with unimpeachable integrity. Not only your conduct but that of the patent office employees as well must be beyond reproach. No hint of impropriety should exist.

Fraud constitutes a knowing misrepresentation by one person to another where it is known that the other person will rely on that faulty information to act to his or her detriment. Fraud has become one of the strong suits of alleged infringers against the charge of infringement and the primary reason for courts to hold that patents are unenforceable or invalid.

Recall that, in the case of Chapter 1 (as in all cases), the patent examiners conducted a full and careful search to uncover all prior art that would have any bearing on the issuance of a patent. Not only is the PTO required to run a search; it is your duty to report all relevant prior art found during any searches conducted by you. Particularly relevant is prior art that an examiner does not locate during his search but is known to you. That is, you may not withhold information on prior art that you believe might be damaging to your chances of receiving a patent if the examiner is made aware of it. The tenor of court rulings has implied that it is fraud not to disclose the relevant prior art that is known to the applicant but not to the examiner. The safe approach appears to be that you should make sure that any prior art that is relevant, or even remotely relevant, to the issuance of a patent, is revealed to the patent office.

Thus, in view of court decisions, it is clear why the standard defense against enforcement action is that the applicant failed to disclose relevant prior art unknown to the PTO. Verification of this fact renders the patent unenforceable or invalid.

5.8.2 Failure to Disclose Technology Already in the Public Domain

If you know that the technology that is the subject of your application was publicly available more than one year prior to your filing but fail to disclose that information to the patent office, you could be guilty of fraud against the patent office. One way you can find yourself in this situation is to place the product on the market one full year before deciding to file your application and to fail to reveal this fact to the PTO. In similar cases the court has held that it is the applicant's duty to advise the PTO as to these facts so that the PTO can decide on patentability.

5.8.3 Arguments Made to the Examiner and the Presentation of Data

You should not make disparaging remarks about the prior art in your application. There are legal reasons why you should not. The inference of various court cases is that presenting strong arguments in favor of patentability of an applicant's invention while downplaying the weak points or facts that mitigate against patentability could work against the applicant.

If you find it necessary to present test data in your application to the PTO, be careful; in some situations, courts have found that presenting favorable data while withholding unfavorable data can constitute fraud. Even though you may select certain data to make a point to the examiner, and withhold data that detract from your point but not in an attempt to deceive, the position of the courts is understandable. You must supply all test data and leave the decision of patentability to the examiner, who thus has adequate information on which to make that decision.

The most important points of these sections are that failure to disclose information, or the selection of certain data over other data, may result in enforcement problems and possible invalidation of your patent if it is ever legally contested. The watchwords are, "Keep your dealings with the PTO beyond reproach." Keep these words in mind.

5.9 DEFENSIVE PUBLICATIONS

There may be occasions when you cannot obtain a patent for an application or just do not want an issued patent, but you would like to prevent someone else from obtaining a patent on the product or process. You need to take steps to make the product or process a prior art reference. To bring this about when you have a pending application, you need to file a paper requesting that:

- An abstract of the disclosure be published.
- The PTO lay the application open to public inspection after publication of the abstract.
- The application be abandoned after a period of five years from the date of application.
- All rights be waived to an enforceable patent based on the application and any continuing application filed 30 months after the initial filing.

However, you retain the right to revive your application if you discover valid reasons, such as the allowance of a patent to someone else for the invention, within the five-year period.

In summary, the three most important pieces of advice I can give you are these. First, study the claims of similar inventions. There is a cerebrally pleasing and stimulating quality to a well-written claim, as with a good work of art. Second, be broad in your claims. Do not limit yourself; leave that task to the examiners—they are skilled at it. And, third, as indicated in Section 5.8, do not create a situation where you can be attacked on the basis of fraud.

6

A Description of Design and Plant Applications and a Discussion of Foreign Patents

The preparation of a design patent application is much simpler than that of a utility application. You will find that the design application either flies with minor objections from the examiner, or it is rejected totally. You cannot narrow the claims or change the drawings because the design is the invention. There is little you can do except point out the differences between your design and prior art if the examiner's objections concern the obviousness of the design. Because the process is so simple, if you develop a distinctive design, you should prepare and file an application for your invention. Do not perform or pay for a thorough search—the effort or cost will be far greater than that spent in preparing the application. A cursory review of journals, popular magazines, and catalogs will suffice as a search. Section 6.1 describes the process.

A plant patent, like a design patent application, requires only one claim and a color drawing or photograph. Section 6.2 gives guidelines for drafting a plant patent application.

Section 6.3 discusses foreign patents.

6.1 GUIDELINES FOR DRAFTING A MODEL DESIGN PATENT

Essentially, the design patent has the same elements as a utility patent. However, it does not include an abstract, a background, or a summary. You are required to provide, in addition to a petition:

- A title.
- A description of the figure(s) of the drawing(s).
- A description of the invention, if any.
- A claim (only one).
- An oath.

The elements of the design patent application are discussed below.

6.1.1 Title

Of the elements in the design patent application, the title ranks first in importance. Hence, great care must be taken in selecting it. The title not only identifies the subject of the design; it also is the name by which the article is known to the public and must be specific. For example, a lamp would be entitled a "lamp" and not "an illumination device." Some latitude is permitted in constructing the title, in that the title "lamp" may be modified by the phrase "... or similar article." The title may particularize the structural type of article or specify its use, for example, "metal lamp" or "reading lamp."

These sample titles reveal that the title should be written in the singular. Also, it should be noted that the design aspects of a utility patent can be the subject of a design patent. The device shown in Figure 4-1 could very well have been not only the subject of a utility patent but also the basis for framing a design patent. However, the design application in a case like this could not be considered a division of the utility application. Thus a design patent application would not have been entitled to the filing date of the utility patent application, even though the drawing of the earlier-filed application showed the same article as that of the design application. In other words, the design patent would have its own filing date.

6.1.2 The Description for a Design Patent

This portion of the application should consist of a brief description of the figures (see Form 2, Appendix A). However, an inventor who feels compelled to add more description—when an appropriate title will not suffice—is permitted a special description that denotes only the aspects of the nature or the environmental uses of the claimed design. Any and all other statements are disallowed and will result in an improper application.

6.1.3 The Claim of the Design Patent

Only one claim is permitted. The claim may include the words: "I claim the ornamental design for a ______ as shown." If there is any descriptive or declaratory matter in the specification other than the brief description or definitions of the drawing figures, the words "and described" must follow "shown." For example, for Figure 4-1, a design patent claim that included no description or declaratory matter in the specification other than a description of the figure would be: "I (we) claim the ornamental design for a drinking cup, substantially as shown."

6.1.4 Drawings

Clearly the heart of the application is the drawings. This point cannot be overemphasized because the drawings constitute substantially the whole disclosure of the design patent. Moreover, an insufficient drawing may be fatal to validity; that is, a lack of completeness in satisfying conditions for patentability at the time of filing can render the application invalid. The requirements that the drawing(s) must meet are given in detail in Appendix D, but owing to the nature of these applications, some amplification is in order. Specifically, the ornamental design that you are claiming must be shown in solid lines in the drawing(s). No shading or broken lines should cross or confuse the appearance of the claimed design. The figures should be shaded appropriately to show character or contours, but remember that it is the article as seen by an observer that is being patented.

Finally, in addition to the drawing you file, it is permissible to include in the application papers a photograph of the article; or, in the case of a flat, thin, article (such as a cloth sample), a sample may be included. Also, in certain cases where the filing date is crucial, you may submit a photograph in lieu of formal drawings. In cases of this nature, the photograph is construed to be a formal drawing so that the application is not ruled incomplete. Once the formal drawing is submitted, the examiner will make a ruling as to whether or not the drawing contains new matter.

6.2 GUIDELINES FOR DRAFTING A MODEL PLANT PATENT APPLICATION

We discussed the scope of *35 U.S.C. 161*, patents for plants, in Section 4.3. In general, the rules that apply to utility patents also apply to plant patents, with two important differences:

- You must file two copies of the application, one of which must be signed and executed (the second copy may be a carbon copy of the original).
- You must submit two copies of color drawings.

You must duplicate the application so that the PTO can pass on one copy to the Department of Agriculture.

6.2.1 Specification

The specification should include a complete, detailed description of the plant and the characteristics thereof that distinguish the same from related known varieties, and its antecedents, expressed in botanical terms in the general form followed in standard botanical textbooks or publications dealing with the varieties of the kind of plant involved (evergreen tree, dahlia plant, rose plant, apple tree, etc.), rather than a mere broad nonbotanical characterization, such as is commonly found in nursery or seed catalogs. The specification should also include the origin or parentage of the plant variety sought to be patented and must particularly point out where and in what manner the variety of plant has been asexually reproduced. Where color is a distinctive feature of the plant, the color should be positively identified in the specification by reference to a designated color as given by a recognized color dictionary.

A plant patent is granted on the entire plant. It therefore follows that only one claim is necessary, and only one is permitted. A method claim in a plant application is improper.

6.2.2 Drawings

Plant patent drawings are not mechanical drawings and should be artistically and competently executed. Figure numbers and reference characters need not be employed unless required by the examiner. The drawing must disclose all the distinctive characteristics of the plant capable of visual representation. The drawing may be in color; and when color is a distinguishing characteristic of the new variety, the drawing must be in color. Two copies of color drawings must be submitted. Color drawings may be made either in permanent watercolor or in oil, or in lieu thereof may be photographs made by color photography or properly colored on sensitized paper. Permanently mounted color photographs are acceptable. The paper in any case must correspond in size, weight, and quality to the paper required for other drawings.

Be sure that, when you mount your color drawings, you leave a two-inch margin at the top. The PTO will use this margin for office markings when the patent is printed.

Depending on the examiner of record, specimens of the plant may be required. In the event of such Herculean requirements, instructions on the packing of specimens will be provided to you. If it is not possible to mail a specimen, a site visit for official inspection can be arranged by representatives of the PTO.

6.3 FOREIGN PATENTS

You know from Chapter 4 that the protection provided by a U.S. patent is valid only throughout the United States and has no effect in a foreign country.

An inventor who wishes to obtain protection within the territorial boundaries of Country A or B must file in each country according to the requirements of that country. This process is best left to experienced professionals. I present it primarily for completeness.

6.3.1 "First to File" Rule of Foreign Patents

A treaty relating to patents is adhered to by 79 countries, including the United States; it is known as the Paris Convention for the Protection of Industrial Property. Under the terms of the treaty, each country guarantees to the citizens of the other countries the same rights in patent and trademark matters that it gives to its own citizens. The treaty also provides for the right of priority in the case of patents, trademarks, and industrial designs (design patents).

This right means that, on the basis of a regular first application filed in one of the member countries, the applicant may, within a certain period of time, approximately six months, apply for protection in all the other member countries. These later applications will then be regarded as if they had been filed on the same day as the first application. Thus, the later applications will have priority over applications for the same invention that may have been filed during the said period of time by other persons. Moreover, these later applications, being based on the first application, will not be invalidated by any acts accomplished in the interval, such as publication or exploitation of the invention, the sale of copies of the design, or use of the trademark.

The period of time mentioned above, within which subsequent applications may be filed in other countries, is twelve months in the case of application for patents and six months in the case of industrial designs and trademarks.

I must caution you that, in practice, you should file in the foreign country six months after the U.S. filing date because a U.S. statute prohibits foreign filing without a special license. This statute is designed to give the U.S. government time to determine whether the application contains information that could be construed to have military significance.

Because foreign patent prosecution and practice is an involved and costly process, you should undertake it only if you feel that your invention has a high probability of being a commercial success outside the United States. The patent laws in many of the foreign countries differ from those of the United States in the length of time that the patent rights are protected. The periods of protection vary from 10 to 15 years from the filing date, rather than 17 years (i.e., utility patent period) from the issue date. In some countries, the inventor must pay annual maintenance fees, which are progressive, or the patent will lapse.

If you wish to file in a foreign country, you may take two possible paths:

- File directly in the countries in which you are interested in securing a patent for your device.
- File under the Patent Corporation Treaty (PCT). Most of the industrial nations of the world have signed this treaty.

I tend to prefer the latter. Filing under the PCT, you avoid having to prepare your application in multiple formats and having to prosecute the same application in several different countries. You may have to pay filing fees in other countries, provide translation of the application into the language of the country, and file an appropriate oath or declaration. But on the average, you save on expenses by filing an international application (under the PCT).

6.3.2 Form of an International Application

Type the application on A4 (29.7 cm × 21 cm) sheets with a top margin on the first sheet of 8 to 9 cm and 2 to 4 cm on subsequent sheets. The left margin should be at least 2.5 to 4 cm. The bottom and right margins should be 2 to 3 cm. Number the sheets consecutively, at the top of the page, and use one-and-one-half-space line spacing.

Number your drawings in separate series, either as 1/3, 2/3, 3/3, or 1, 2, 3. You must place a drawing on size A4 paper (26.2 cm × 17 cm) that is flexible, strong, white, smooth, nonshining, and durable. The figures should not exceed (26.2 cm × 17 cm), and one (of the figures) should be designed for use on the front page. The front page figure should characterize the invention. These minor changes comprise all the differences between a U.S. application and a PCT application.

6.3.3 How to File a PCT Application

You can file under the PCT if your U.S. application met the above requirements. To do so, however, you must obtain a request (Form PCT/RO/101) and a transmittal letter (Form PTO 1382) from Box PCT, Patent and Trademark Office, Washington, D.C. 20231. These forms are used to request that the PTO prepare a certified copy of your U.S. application for use with the PCT application and to transmit your filing fees as indicated on Form PCT/RO/101.

The basic flow of the application is determined by the countries you have designated for patent protection. The date of your U.S. application is the date for determining priority. At your request, the Receiving Office prepares and transmits a copy of the international application, called the search copy, to the International Searching Authority (ISA) and a record copy to the International Bureau (IB). A third copy is retained by the Receiving Office.

The ISA prepares a search report, which contains a listing of those documents found to be relevant and the claims in the application to which they pertain. The ISA does not make any judgment about patentability. The search report is forwarded to the IB and to the applicant. The IB function is to maintain the master file of international applications. If you have not filed a certified copy of your application in the Receiving Office with the international application, or requested that the Receiving Office prepare and transmit to the IB a copy of the prior U.S. national application, you must submit a certified copy to the IB not later than 16 months after the U.S. filing date. You have two months from the date of transmittal of the search report to the IB to amend the claims by filing directly with the IB. At the expiration of 18 months from the priority date, the IB will publish the application, the search report, and any amendments in pamphlet form. Copies of these pamphlets are transmitted to the countries where you are seeking protection.

Twenty months from the priority date of the international application, you must send to each country any required translations and the appropriate national or regional filing fees unless the time period is extended. You can amend your application within one month of payment of your national fees, but after this period each country will make its own decision about patentability under its own national or regional laws.

I did not discuss how one would go about filing directly with a foreign country because I have not attempted that process. Furthermore, the process is so complicated that some patent attorneys use their own intermediaries, namely law firms that specialize in foreign patents, to handle their foreign filing.

7

Innovation

Frequently, we employ the term innovation synonymously with the word invention, when in fact invention is only part of the process. As we have discussed before, invention has a precise legal meaning. It has two defined steps, starting with Step 1, the conception of an idea. The second and last step is reduction to practice.

Once Step 1 has occurred, you must be diligent in your effort to reduce the concept to practice. The type of effort, on the inventor's part, that constitutes diligence has been the subject of legal analysis, and defined by legions of lawyers. In your case, it suffices to say that, from the moment you have the idea, you must expend some effort to move the idea from the conceptual stage to final conclusion—reduction to practice. Otherwise, if anyone ever contests your invention, a legal question can arise as to claims of who was first.

Reduction to practice is accomplished by "actual" and "constructive" reduction to practice. "Actual" refers to the physical realization of an idea, whereas "constructive" means the preparation and filing of a patent application in the U.S. PTO. However, after the "constructive" reduction to practice, the real fun begins in the innovation process.

7.1 THE INNOVATION PROCESS

The innovation process consists of those myriad steps that take place beyond the achievement of the invention. Those actions fall under the heading of commercialization. You can expect to spend much more effort in commercializing your invention than you put into developing it. The effort of commercialization frequently provides valuable feedback to the inventor, and some of this feedback may change the initial idea or the product.

It would be presumptuous to try to tell anyone how to invent, although there are numerous so-called creative thinking techniques. This book does not attempt to cover those strategies, but I would like to share with you insights I have gained on how best to handle invention-related subject matter that surfaces because of the development effort or observations.

I have found it good to assume that inventors create new ideas in response to actual needs. This is true whether you are a casual or a professional inventor, working alone or in a large organization. I have also seen that successful inventing is based on well-defined objectives and a clear definition of the need you wish to fill. Results happen when you identify specific problem areas that match your capabilities, your technology interests, and your expertise. Do not develop a solution and then look for a problem.

The process, shown in Figure 7-1, is a simple, orderly procedure that is used by many professional inventors to assure that any resulting inventions:

- Satisfy a substantial market need.
- Are feasible to produce.
- Meet company or personal objectives.

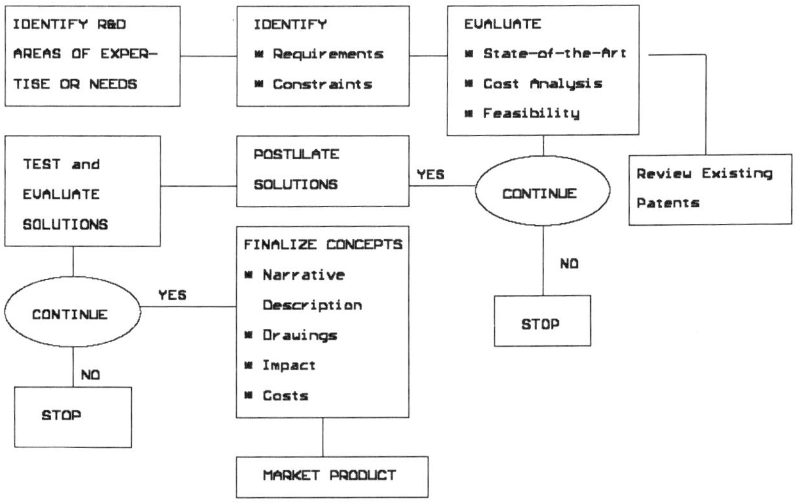

FIGURE 7-1. A Schematic Representation of the Innovation Process

Let me repeat an earlier observation. No one can tell anyone how to invent, but if a person possesses inventive capabilities, I can suggest how to apply them for the benefit of society and profit to the innovator.

The most important feature of this proposed process is that you consider the business aspects *early* in the innovation cycle.

7.2 MARKETING ASPECTS OF THE INNOVATION PROCESS

The majority of innovations never see the commercial market. However, most of these innovations, contrary to popular belief, do not fail because they are without merit; they fail because of factors not related to their merits. If these factors are recognized or detected early in the process, the knowledge gained can make the difference between success and failure—or at least prevent serious financial losses.

For example, a device was developed by a small company for use in fossil power plants. The company learned from its authoritative source that there was a need for the device throughout the fossil industry; but to avoid exposure of the device—believing it would be difficult to get a strong patent position for it—the company did not talk to decision makers in the industry. That is, it did not do a market survey to determine:

1. Acceptability of products from untested companies.
2. Promotion requirements needed to promote the advantages, features, and benefits of the device.
3. Existing resistance by competitors against market encroachment.

The company believed very strongly that it understood:

4. Societal factors, which in this case were minimal (factors such as safety, environmental impact, and product liability).
5. Investment cost for research and development; profitability, payback period, potential market, need (demand), distribution, and service requirements.

It happened that even though the company understood items 4 and 5, items 1, 2, and 3 were just too much to overcome. The firm finally abandoned the product, with a considerable loss of money. The message is very clear—do some market research to understand the effect of items 1 through 5 before you are too far down the road.

Your market review should produce data on variables (potential problems) such as:

- Characteristics of the market you are after.
- Resistance to new products.
- The intensity of competition in your targeted market.
- Marketing schemes that might be effective, including product design, pricing, and promotional requirements.
- Potential problems, such as legal, technical, and environmental problems that might mitigate against commercialization.
- Volatility of the market.
- Potential sales and profitability, with all cost and contingencies factored into your projections.

Careful consideration of all these points will not guarantee success, but at least it will minimize the potential for serious mistakes.

By way of example, let us consider the case of an inventor whose objectives and expertise have directed him into areas of passive solar collection. The inventor has the technical interest and expertise, and has assessed the marketing opportunities in this field. He knows the current technology of passive solar techniques, especially those using flat plate collectors.

The inventor is familiar with the analog circuits and hardware and plumbing design. His latest work has centered around the use of single-plate flat plate collectors filled with carbon dioxide gas. The gas is transparent to the incident solar radiation but opaque to long-wavelength thermal radiation emitted from the surface of the absorber in the collector. The carbon dioxide acts to trap the long wavelength thermally emitted by the absorber in the collector. It thus reduces the need for multiplates in the collector.

The inventor has identified two areas of home and residential energy needs where his collector has an impact:

- Hot water heating.
- Space heating.

These two areas need to be considered separately. Suppose we concentrate on hot water heating. This problem must be analyzed further to determine the requirements for a new system for heating water in homes.

The average home hot water heating cost is found to be $200 to $300 a year; so that is all that can be saved by a passive solar hot water heater. At current prices—approximately $1500 to 2000 for a "turn-key" passive solar hot water heating system—it will take six years or more to recover the initial installation cost of a solar hot water system.

A new system, to be successful in the marketplace, must meet the following requirements:

- *Cost*: it must not exceed $1000 in cost at the home-owner level.
- *Maintainability*: it must have low maintenance cost and a long life; it should have a minimum number of parts.

- *Functionality*: it must be simple to operate and use.
- *Liability*: it must be safe.
- *Societal*: it must have no environmental impact and must be aesthetically pleasing.

An examination of the state of the art will show that it is indeed feasible to design and market an effective solar-heated hot water heater for residential use that meets the above requirements. The review of the state of the art, including a preliminary patent search, revealed that a collector using carbon dioxide had not been patented. The search suggested that some patent protection could be obtained. It was time to move to the design phase.

7.3 PRELIMINARY DESIGN

The system must be simple in design to achieve low cost and low maintenance, and still must be durable enough to attract users.

The requirements developed above can form the basis for various system designs that are usable for management and control functions. The first steps in laying out design concepts are to identify functional requirements and problems with existing solar hot water systems, to estimate the cost of major items, and to examine the basic parameters to be considered. This process shows the limiting factors and highlights the areas where improvements are needed; that is, it identifies the weaknesses of existing systems. At this point, it is reasonable to make conceptual designs using purely idealized components or systems.

To conclude the preliminary design effort, describe the best concepts in a brief narrative and include the cost estimates and designs. The preliminary design should serve as the basis for all decisions regarding whether to proceed with or to abandon the project.

7.4 EVALUATION

It is necessary to evaluate the preliminary design concepts to ensure that they satisfy the specified requirements and represent a viable product in the marketplace.

The first task is to carry out a technical evaluation. If you cannot perform the technical evaluation, find other sources of opinion, such as trusted consultants, friends, and others in the field. The problem with this approach is the fear that you are unnecessarily exposing proprietary ideas that might be stolen! Before you submit an idea to a second party, try to get the second party to sign a proprietary information agreement. At least be sure to include a proprietary information agreement with any disclosure. Figure 7-2 shows a sample proprietary agreement form.

If you are an independent inventor, technical evaluation can be more difficult. Rarely does an independent inventor have available the talent needed for evaluation, the testing equipment, or the money to hire or buy them. If you lack these resources, you need to know where to go for help.

In the energy field, the Federal Nonnuclear Research and Development Act of 1974 (Public Law 93-577) established a comprehensive national program for research and development of all potentially beneficial energy sources and utilization technologies. This program is conducted by the Department of Energy (DOE) (see Table 7-1). The purpose of the program is to provide an opportunity for independent small businesses and inventors

Proprietary Information Agreement

__________________ (Recipient) acknowledges that the attached document(s) entitled:

____ contain valuable

proprietary information of ____________________________ and understands that

these documents and the information contained thereon are therefore furnished to Recipient under the following conditions:

1. The documents and the information contained thereon shall be used solely for evaluating a proposal from or supplying a quotation or component to ______________________.

2. Recipient agrees not to disclose these documents or the information thereon to any person outside recipient's organization or to any person within recipient's organization not having a bona fide "need to know" same.

3. Recipient shall exercise due care to safeguard these documents and the information contained thereon or derived therefrom from access by unauthorized persons.

These terms shall not apply to any information which Recipient can document was in or enters the public domain without fault of Recipient or was in or comes into recipient's possession without restriction.

______________________ ______________________

Date Recipient

FIGURE 7-2. Sample Proprietary Information Agreement

TABLE 7.1. Where to Seek Assistance to Inventors and Innovators

Agency	Area of Support/Function
National Science Foundation (NSF) 1800 G. Street, N.W Washington, DC 20550 (202) 632-5728	The NSF promotes scientific research through an extensive grant program. Grants are given primarily for basic scientific research aimed at improving the quality of life through the creation of new processes and products. The NSF *Guide to Programs* should be consulted.
National Bureau of Standards (NBS) Office of Energy Related Inventions (OERI) Department of Commerce Washington, DC 20234 (202) 921-1000	NBS is presently operating the Energy-Related Invention Evaluation Program aimed at encouraging innovation in developing non-nuclear technology. The program evaluates all promising energy-related inventions. Interested parties should write to OERI for a complete information packet.
Department of Energy Energy Invention Support Program Office Washington, DC 20585 (202) 252-5000	Program is operated by NBS's Office of Energy-Related Inventions.
Invention Branch Room 8 G031 (202) 256-6260	Acts as a clearinghouse for information on all types of financial, technical, and administrative assistance available to inventors and innovators. Provides referals to other federal agencies.
Unsolicited Proposals Sections Department of Energy 400 1st Street, N.W. Washington, DC 20585 (202) 376-9203	This office is the DOE focal point for receiving and recording unsolicited energy-related proposals; assigns a DOE ID Number to each proposal and forwards it to the appropriate DOE office. Inventors unaccustomed to writing formal unsolicited proposals may contact DOE's Invention Branch.
National Oceanic Atmospheric Administration National Sea Grant Program Department of Commerce 6010 Executive Blvd. Rockville, MD 20852 (301) 443-8243	Offers grants to companies and institutions for marine research.
Special Projects Division Office of Finance Small Business Administration 1441 L Street, N.W. Washington, DC 20416 (202) 653-6696	Through regional offices, provides direct loans up to $350,000 and loan guarantees up to $500,000 to help small businesses market inventions. Areas of interest are solar conversions, cogeneration, and wind energy equipment.
U.S. Small Business Administration Office of Innovation, Research and Technology Mail Code: 6470 409 Third Street, S.W. Washington, DC 20416	At least twelve major Federal agencies are involved in this program. Contract opportunities are announced each year by participating Federal agencies.

with promising energy-related inventions to obtain federal assistance in developing and commercializing their inventions. The average award is $70,000.

Any new concept, device, product, material, or industrial process qualifies. The invention need not be patented. The invention should be well described on paper; drawings are encouraged but need not be done professionally. Claims should be set forth clearly, pointing out how the invention is unique, how its performance costs are advantageous over those of similar items on the market or in development, and how the invention will affect national energy objectives. The basis for the claims (for example, calculations or test data) must be included.

Another resource is the group of Invention Evaluation Centers set up at several universities by the Experimental Research and Development Program of the National Science Foundation. One of these centers is the Experimental Center for the Advancement of Invention and Innovation established by the College of Business Administration at the University of Oregon, Eugene, Oregon.

You may also consider trading an interest in your invention for professional services in a technical area. Your lawyer, accountant, marketing researcher, or general business advisor might barter his or her services in the hope of enjoying future profits with you.

In assessing any difficulties of commercialization, you need to evaluate the entire design, including hardware and software. Factors that might contribute to such difficulties include:

- Manufacturability
- Quality control
- Maintainability
- Durability
- Human factors
- Proprietary design protection

Record the results of this evaluation, and make appropriate changes to the design concept.

7.5 THE FINAL DESIGN CONCEPT

Document carefully the final design concept, which now includes any revisions. The documentation should consist of narrative descriptions, physical layout drawings, and schematics. Include in the description cost estimates, manufacturing methods, and the preliminary engineering design plan and costs. The documented design concept requires special handling to guard any proprietary information, and in many cases is the basis for a patent application. If so, attend to this matter promptly to protect against undesired disclosure to outside sources.

The above processes of postulating solutions can be used for any identified problem area, with any type of product or service. The example used is, of course, very specific, but it illustrates the nature of the basic innovative process. Many inventors use a pragmatic approach, and this may work well in some cases; but for many inventors the procedure outlined above results in a more practical invention, as it addresses the business aspects of the product in the early stages.

7.6 THE OPTIMIZING PROCESS

You will need to decide whether you will develop, license, sell, or commercialize your innovation. If the innovation requires neither technology development nor engineering and design efforts, you must decide whether to attempt commercialization yourself or to seek sales/licensing arrangements.

If the product requires further research and development (R&D), there are five alternatives:

1. Use your own capital.
2. Obtain financing from private sources.
3. Borrow from a bank.
4. Interest a venture capital firm in advancing funds, in which case you will have to give up part of your ownership.
5. Seek government funding.

Alternatives 1, 2, and 3 risk the loss of capital or incurring personal debt, but they provide the best protection for the idea.

Alternative 4 reduces the risk of capital loss and also provides proprietary safeguards, but you will have to relinquish part of your ownership. Facing this, weigh the pros and cons of alternative sources of development funds. The important considerations are:

1. Is performance of the work without federal funds the only means of protecting future marketing prospects?
2. Will this independent effort enhance sales and licensing options?
3. Will ultimate commercialization of the product be easier to achieve as a result of not using federal funds?
4. Can you substantially reduce the time necessary for development work if you are not delayed by waiting for federal contracts to be negotiated, approved, and funded?

Alternative 5 eliminated most of the risk in capital losses and personal debt. There are, however, some disadvantages. There is the possibility that the work will become public knowledge unless you can obtain a specific agreement covering proprietary interests, and this is not easy. Nor is it easy to work with federal contracts. They require considerable paperwork, and compliance with numerous regulations covering personnel, accounting records, and government property. Furthermore, persons using government funds are subject to special government auditing in addition to Internal Revenue Service audits. The entire procedure for obtaining federal funds is time-consuming and involves lengthy waiting periods during which your proposal moves through the bureaucratic paper mill. Terms of contract must be negotiated after your proposal is approved, and an additional period of waiting follows until the contract funds are approved, the contract papers are prepared, and all of the government personnel concerned sign off.

The primary aim in any case is to minimize your potential risk. The final chapter of this book provides techniques for examining the economic risk. The other risk factors were covered in Section 7.2.

7.7 FINALLY, LOOK AT YOURSELF BEFORE YOU LEAP

To avoid a serious mistake, you must not only be a good innovator, but you must have management skills (or know where to find them) in order to act on the information you have at hand. Poor management is one reason among many why commercially feasible products fail.

Table 7-2 is a worksheet developed by the Small Business Administration. You should rate yourself to see whether you have the personal traits needed by the proprietor of a business. The various personality traits are ranked from a high of 4 down to a low of 1. If you believe that you fall between one of the ordered phrases, score yourself accordingly. A score of 30 means that you possess the necessary personal traits to be a good entrepreneur; that is, as long as you cannot find a personal trait in the Rank 1 column. Having a Rank 1 trait should be a signal to you to seek a partner who does not possess that trait.

TABLE 7-2. Rating Scale for Evaluating Personal Traits Important to the Proprietor of a Business

Rank Score	4	3	2	1
Initiative	Additional tasks sought; highly ingenious	Resourceful; alert to opportunities	Regular work performed without waiting for directions	Routine worker awaiting directions
Attitude toward others	Positive; friendly interest in people	Pleasant, polite	Sometimes difficult to work with	Inclined to be quarrelsome or uncooperative
Leadership	Forceful, inspiring confidence and loyalty	Order giver	Driver	Weak
Responsibility	Responsibility sought and welcomed	Accepted without protest	Unwilling to assume without protest	Avoided whenever possible
Organizing ability	Highly capable of perceiving and arranging fundamentals in logical order	Able organizer	Fairly capable of organizing	Poor organizer
Industry	Industrious; capable of working hard for long hours	Can work hard, but not for too long a period	Fairly industrious	Hard work avoided
Decision	Quick and accurate	Good and careful	Quick, but often unsound	Hesitant and fearful
Sincerity	Courageous, square-shooter	On the level	Fairly sincere	Inclined to lack sincerity
Perseverance	Highly steadfast in purpose; not discouraged by obstacles	Effort steadily maintained	Average determination and persistence	Little or no persistence
Physical energy	Highly energetic at all times	Energetic most of the time	Fairly energetic	Below average

8

Other Considerations, Infringement, and Validity

A water fountain joke about patents is that: a patent and fifty cents will get you a cup of coffee. This put-down may no longer be appropriate, however. In recent years, there has been an increasing number of highly publicized court decisions decided in favor of patentees. Knowing this, you should, if awarded a patent, protect your property. This chapter discusses various things you should know about patents.

8.1 YOUR PATENT: WHAT GOOD IS IT?

Your patent, depending on its type (i.e., design, utility, or plant), provides you the right to take legal action against anyone who makes, uses, or sells your invention during the 17-year term of the patent. If you find an infringer and have to sue, the suit, if successful, allows you to recover damages for the period covered by the patent—extending back six years from the date you filed suit. It also, if successful, will allow you to get an injunction preventing the infringer from using your invention in the future or during the remaining life of the patent. Unless you can show that the infringer's conduct was willful (flagrant or in bad faith), the damages you get are equivalent to a reasonable royalty that you would have received had the infringer approached you in good faith about making your invention.

The patent is personal property and should be treated as such. You can hang it on your den wall, or you can try to make it work for you. To make it work for you, you also must protect it against infringers, people, and companies that would try to take it away from you. Protecting your rights involves your being able to recognize when they are being abused; that is, you must know enough to spot an infringer and get yourself a lawyer. Other ways in which you can lose the exclusive rights provided under U.S. patent laws also are discussed below.

8.2 INFRINGEMENT

A company or a person legally infringes your patent by making, using, or selling a product that contains all the elements of your patented invention within the territory of the United States during the active life of the invention without authorization. There are several basic tests of patent infringement that you can use to review a product that you believe contains or embodies your invention:

- Does the device meet all the elements of the main claim of your patent?
- Does the device meet all the elements of the main claim or their equivalents?
- Is the device equivalent to your invention in structure and function, and does it produce the same results as your invention?
- Is the device useful only in the device defined by your patent?

Consider the hypothetical case of an invention with independent claims 1 and 2. If a product meets all the elements of claim 1 but not 2, it infringes. Or consider the hypothetical case of an invention with an independent claim containing elements A, B, C, and D. If a device is defined by elements A, C, and D, it does not meet all the elements of the claim. However, if it contains the elements A, B, C, D, E, and F, it infringes. It is not important that it contains elements E and F; by containing elements A, B, C, and D, it satisfies the first infringement test. Or if it contains elements A and B plus the equivalents of C and D, it satisfies the second test, and in fact infringes on the hypothetical patent.

As an example, I have reproduced below the independent claim from one of my patents (Patent Number 4,277,727) entitled "A Digital Room Light Controller." The main claim reads:

1. Apparatus for turning a light on when a person enters an unoccupied room and maintaining a net count equal to the difference between the number of persons entering and leaving the room so as to automatically maintain the room light in an on position when the total count is greater than zero or to maintain the room light in an off position when the total count is zero comprising: three light beam emitters that broadcast three parallel light beams; three light beam sensors positioned in said doorways so as to sense an interruption of one or more said light beams transmitted thereto;

electronic means cooperating with each one of said sensors for emitting a pulse of electric current for each interruption of each said light beams; electronic means for generating an electrical signal of finite duration in response to each said pulse of electric current; electronic means for processing said signals so as to produce a first output pulse only when said signals are generated in a first predetermined sequence and for producing a second output pulse only when said signals are generated in a second predetermined sequence; an up-down counter for counting said output pulses having the first output pulse applied to its Up input terminal and the second output pulse applied to its Down input terminal; and, electronic means for decoding the accumulated count stored in said counter and controlling the on/off state of the room lights in accordance therewith.

The elements of this claim are:

A Three light beam emitters.
B Three light beam sensors.
C Electronic means for emitting a pulse of electric current for each beam interruption.
D Electronic means for generating an electrical signal for each electric pulse element.
E Electronic means for processing these signals.
F Up-down counter for counting processed signals.
G Electronic means for decoding the accumulated count.

You could clear this prior art if you build a device with a new element, B', not equivalent to B while retaining the remaining six elements; or if you build a device with an element F' removing the need for element G, where, for example F' is a microprocessor controller with firmware for maintaining the count of the people in a room and an onboard electronic means for controlling the off/on state of the room light, then the device with this F' element will, in my opinion, not infringe on my patent.

The last two tests or questions are not so transparent. The third question (test), if answered yes, implies that this device infringes under the "doctrine of equivalents." The last test relates to what is called the doctrine of "contributory infringement." For example, take a utility patent for timing automobiles, where the method for timing automobiles requires the use of a visible blue light laser diode transmitter–photodiode receiver unit with a special integral adapter in combination with a microcomputer with a special signal conditioning and analysis means. If the blue light laser diode transmitter–photodiode receiver unit with its special adapter is manufactured by company A and sold to company B, which makes a microcomputer with a signal conditioning and analysis means substantially equivalent to that of your patent, and the combination is used to time automobiles, then companies A and B may be liable for "contributory infringement."

To check for infringement, you will need to gather all the information available on the device thought to be infringing. This information should include manuals, brochures, advertisements, photographs, and so on. Acquire the infringing device so that you can disassemble it and study it in detail. The legal cost of pursuing an infringer can be prohibitive. However, if you believe your patent is being infringed, see a lawyer.

After reading the above discussion, two things should be clear to you. You should:

- Use means (broad) claims whenever possible.
- Try to reduce the number of elements whenever possible.

The fewer the elements, the more difficult it becomes to avoid the patent.

Finally, be aware that today the vast majority of patents granted are merely improvements or refinements on a basic invention. The claims allowed in a basic patent are always broad when compared to those allowed in an improvement patent. Improvement patents are most vulnerable to attack by people who want to make your device.

8.3 VALIDITY

Validity is implied by patentability. However, if your invention is commercially viable, it will be subjected to a validity test by others—the people who want to nudge you out of possession! The examiner is not going to be primarily concerned with validity; so you had better see that all loopholes are closed. The Patent Office examiners are taxed very heavily with cases. They can overlook prior art that would make many patents unpatentable.

Patents are invalid if it can be shown that:

- The PTO missed certain prior art references in its review of the patent application.
- The device described in the application is inoperable.
- The claims are vague and indefinite.
- The application is incomplete.

Finally, on the subject of validity, on July 1, 1981, it became law that all unexpired U.S. patents and some already expired could be challenged. The validity of any patent granted within the last 23 years can be challenged merely by paying a fee and explaining why the patent should be reexamined. A successful challenge may result in the cancellation of one or more claims made in the patent. It remains to be seen whether this statute can improve the quality and reliability of issued patents or whether it will work to the disadvantage of small companies and lone inventors. Remember that it is up to you to ensure against this kind of encroachment by others. There is no point in getting an indefensible patent.

Go beyond the ideas close to yours; do not just look at devices that are similar to your own. If you have conceived of a new device to mix foods, you need to consider devices used to mix concrete or other industrial products.

8.4 INTERFERENCE

We inventors always worry when working on a new device that somewhere there is someone else working on the same device who may be the first to reduce it to practice. If such a person exists, here is what happens if our patent applications are filed essentially at the same time. According to 37 CFR 1.201:

a) an interference is a proceeding instituted for the purpose of determining the question of priority of invention between two or more parties claiming substantially the same patentable invention and may be instituted as soon as it is determined that common patentable subject matter is claimed in a plurality of applications or in an application and a patent.
b) an interference will be declared between pending applications for patent, or for reissue, of different parties when such applications contain claims for substantially the same invention, which are allowable in the application of each party, and interferences will also be declared between pending applications for patent, or for reissue, and unexpired original or reissued patents, of different parties, when such applications and patents contain claims for substantially the same invention which are allowable in all of the applications involved, in accordance with the provisions of these rules.

Even if a patent claiming substantially the same invention as that of a pending application has been issued, an interference can be declared within one year of the issue date.

The PTO will declare an interference whenever an application is submitted that, in its opinion, would interfere with any pending application or unexpired patent. The question of priority of invention is then determined by a board of patent interferences. The winner will be the first to reduce his or her invention to practice (i.e., file application, build and test the invention; see Chapter 2), or the first to conceive it and to show that he or she has been diligent in his or her effort to reduce the invention to practice. To do this you must show that the issued patent and your pending application are claiming the same invention. One way to accomplish this is to present the claims of the patent in your application, making both sets of claims identical. Or you might do this by copying the claims of the patent in your pending application, identifying the patent to the examiner, and showing by argument that your application supports the claims of the issued patent. A large proportion of interferences with a patent arise via the initiative of the applicant in copying claims of a patent that has come to his or her attention through citation in an office action or otherwise. Remember, however, that this action can be taken against a patent issued to you.

8.5 WHAT OFFICE ACTIONS CAN BE APPEALED

As the PTO makes many decisions of a discretionary nature, most applicants will at some point feel denied patent protection to which they are entitled. When differences of opinion result in denial of patent claims because of prior art and material deficiencies in the application, the applicant may petition the Commissioner of the PTO. In those instances, if the applicant's claims have been rejected twice or he or she has been given a final rejection, the applicant may, for a fee, appeal the decision of the examiner to the Board of Appeals within the time for response allotted by the examiner.

8.6 FEES

In the brief time that I have been involved in the patenting process the fees for participating in every facet of this process have increased. The basic filing fees for utility, design, and plant applications have continued to increase. The fees shown in Appendix B were effective as of December 16, 1991. The cost of filing an application will continue to rise. Given the cost of securing patent protection for your invention, you should carefully consider the risk and benefits of filing your application. If you decide to do it yourself, do not hesitate to seek help from a professional if you get in over your head.

Appendix A

Forms of Petitions, Oaths, or Declarations and Others

Form 1
Sample Transmittal Letter for Patent Application

____
Date

Commissioner of Patents and Trademarks
Washington, District of Columbia 20231

Sir:

Attached for filing are the following patent application papers.

Inventor(s): ______________________________

Title: ______________________________

____

Pages of Specification and Claims: ______________________________

Sheets of Drawings: ______________________________

Date Application was signed: ______________________________

					Base Fee =	$345
Total Claims	______	– 20 =	______		x $10 =	______
Independent Claims	______	–3 =	______		x $36 =	______
Check Enclosed for Total:						______

Very respectfully,

________________	________________
Signature of Inventor #2	Signature of Inventor #1
________________	________________
Typed Name of Inventor #2	Typed Name of Inventor #1
________________	________________
Address	Address
________________	________________

Form 2
Sample Design Patent Application Petition

Commissioner of Patents
Washington, District of Columbia 20231

Sir:

The undersigned petitioner(s) pray(s) that letters patent may be granted to the undersigned for the new and original design set forth in the following specification. The Filing Fee of $140 is attached.

Specification

Be it known that the undersigned inventor(s) has (have) invented a new, original,

and ornamental design entitled"_______________________________________"
Title

Of which the following is a specification, reference being made to the accompanying drawing(s), forming a part hereof.

Fig. 1 is a ______________________
Type of view

Fig. 2 is a ______________________
Type of view

I (we) claim the ornamental design for a ____________________________

____ as shown.
Title of design

____
Signature

____
Signature

You must include a declaration with this petition. The declaration is given on the following page.

Form 3
Sample Declaration

Declaration

The undersigned petitioner(s) declare(s) that she, he, or they is or are citizen(s) of the United States and residents of ______________________ and
City and State
______________________ respectively, that he, she, or they verily believe(s)
City and State
herself, himself, or themselves to be the original, first, and sole/joint inventor(s) of the design entitled " ______________________
Title
described and claimed in the foregoing specification; that she, he, or they do(es) not know and do(es) not believe that the same was ever known or used in the United States before her, his, or their invention thereof, or patented or described in printed publication in any country before her, his, or their invention thereof, or more than one year prior to this application, or in public use or sale in the United States more than one year prior to this application; that said design has not been patented in any country foreign to the United States on an application filed by her, his, or their legal representatives or assigns more than six months prior to this application; and that no application for patent on said design has been filed by her, his, or their representatives or assigns in any country foreign to the United States. The undersigned petitioner(s) declare(s) further that all statements made herein of her, his, or their own knowledge are true and that all statements made on information and belief are believed to be true; and further that these statements were

(Continued)

Form 3
Sample Declaration *(continued)*

made with the knowledge that willful false statements and the like so made are punishable by fine or imprisonment, or both, under Title 18, U.S. Code, Sec. 1001, and that such willful false statements may jeopardize the validity of this application or any patent issuing thereon.

____________________	____________________
Date	Signature
	____________________
	Typed Name
Send correspondence to:	____________________
	Address
	____________________
	____________________
	Signature
	____________________
	Typed Name
	____________________
	Address
	____________________

* Note that this declaration does not have to be notarized.

Form 4
Sample Petition and Oath for a Plant Patent

Commissioner of Patents
Washington, D.C. 20231

Sir:

Your petitioner, ____________________________, a citizen of the United States and a resident of ________________, State of ____________________, prays that letters patent may be granted to him for the new and distinct variety of _____ ______________________________ set forth in the following specifications:

(The specification, which includes the description of the invention and the claims, is included between the above petition and the following oath.)

____________________, the above-named petitioner, being sworn (or affirmed), deposes and says that he is a citizen of the United States and a resident of _______ ___________, State of ________________, and he verily believes himself to be the original, first and sole inventor of the new and distinct variety of _________ _________________________ described and claimed in the foregoing specifications; that he has asexually reproduced the said new and distinct variety; that he does not know and does not believe that the same was ever known or used before his invention thereof, or patented or described in any printed publication in any country before his invention thereof, or more than one year prior to this application, or in public use or on sale in the United States more than one year prior to this application; that said invention has not been patented or made the subject of an inventor's certificate in any country foreign to the United States on an application filed by him or his legal representative or assigns more than twelve months prior to this application; that he acknowledges his duty to disclose information of

(Continued)

Form 4
Sample Petition and Oath for a Plant Patent *(continued)*

which he is aware which is material to the examination of this application; and that no application for patent or said invention has been filed by him or his representatives or assigns in any country foreign to the United States, except as follows:

____

____
Inventor's full signature

State of ______________________

ss:

Sworn to and subscribed before me this ______ day of ______________, 19___

____
Signature of notary or officer

(SEAL)

____
Official character

Form 5
Request for Certificate of Correction in the United States Patent and Trademark Office

Patent No.:

Issued

Request for Certificate of Correction

Date ______________

Commissioner of Patents and Trademarks
Washington, District of Columbia 20231

Sir:

1. The above patent contains significant error, as indicated on the attached Certificate of Correction form (submitted in duplicate). These errors arose at the respective places in the application file indicated below.
2. Since such error arose through the fault of the Patent and Trademark Office, it is requested that the Certificate be issued at no cost to applicant.
3. Such error arose through the fault of the applicant(s). A check for the $70 fee is enclosed. Such error is of a clerical or minor nature and occurred in good faith and therefore issuance of the Certificate of Correction is respectfully requested.

Specifically,

Mailing Address of Sender: Patent No. __________

Form 6
United States Patent and Trademark Office Certificate of Correction

Patent No.:

Dated:

Inventor(s):

It is certified that error appears in the above-identified patent and that said Letters Patent are hereby corrected as shown below:

Form 7
Sample Certificate of Mailing

To: The Commissioner of Patents and Trademarks
Washington, DC 20231

Certificate of Mailing

I hereby certify that this correspondence is being deposited with the United States Postal Service as first class mail in an envelope addressed to: Commissioner of Patents and Trademarks, Washington, D.C. 20231, on ________________(Date).

Name of Applicant:

Signature:

Date:

Form 8
Sample Form: The Continuation Petition in the United States Patent and Trademark Office

Date

Commissioner of Patents and Trademarks
Washington, District of Columbia 20231

Sir:

1. Please prepare a ( ) Continuation/( ) Divisional application under Rule 60 of pending prior application of _______________(Inventor(s)), Ser. No. ____________, filed ___________, 19___, titled "_________ __________________." Said prior application was in charge of Examiner ________________________ in G.A.U. ___________________.
2. Please prepare a copy of the prior application.
3. Please cancel all claims of the prior application, except Claim 1.
4. A check for the filing fee of $345 for one independent claim is enclosed.
5. Please amend the specification by inserting before the first line the sentence—This is a ( ) Continuation/( )Division of application Ser. No. ______________, filed ______________, 19___.

( )6a. Transfer the drawing(s) from the prior application (base issue fee has not been paid) to this application and abandon said prior application as of the filing date of this application. A duplicate of this sheet is enclosed for insertion in the file of the prior application.

( )6b. New formal drawing(s) (_____ sheets) are (is) enclosed.

7. A preliminary amendment is enclosed. (Claim numbering begins with next number after highest numbered claim of prior application.) The undersigned declare(s) further that all statements made herein of his/her/their own knowledge are true and that all statements made on information and belief are believed to be true; and further that these statements were made with the knowledge that willful false statements and the like so made are punishable by fine or imprisonment, or both, under Section 1001 of Title 18 of the U.S. Code and that such willful false statements may jeopardize the validity of the application or any patent issuing thereon.

Correspondent's Name and Address

Form 9
Statement of Prior Art In the United States Patent and Trademark Office

Inventor(s):

Serial No. Group Art Unit:

Filed: Examiner:

Title:

Statement of Prior Art

Commissioner of Patents and Trademarks
Washington, D.C. 20231

Sir:

The prior art listed below has come to the attention of applicant(s). This prior art is believed relevant to, but patentably distinguishable from, the present invention and is being cited pursuant to Rule 97. A copy of each prior-art publication is enclosed and its relevance is discussed below.

Form 10
Letter Requesting Participation in the PTO Disclosure Document Program

(Date)

Applicant: Examiner:

Serial No.: Group Art Unit:

Filed:

For:

Commissioner of Patents and Trademarks
Washington, D.C. 20231

Request for Participation in
Disclosure Document Program:
Disclosure of (Your Name)

Entitled (Title of Disclosure)

Sir:

I have attached a disclosure of my above-entitled invention (consisting of _____ sheets of written description and ______ separate drawings or photos), a $10 check, a stamped, addressed return envelope, and a duplicate copy of this letter.

It is hereby respectfully requested that this disclosure be accepted and retained for two years under the Disclosure Document Program.

Very respectfully,

____
Your signature

____
Print name

____
Address

____

Enclosures: As stated above

Form 11
Disclosure Document Reference Letter in the United States Patent and Trademark Office

Ser. No.: ______________________________

Filed: ______________________________

Inventor(s): ______________________________

Title: ______________________________

Group Art Unit: ______________________________

Examiner: ______________________________

Disclosure Document Reference Letter

Commissioner of Patents and Trademarks
Washington, D.C. 20231

Sir:

The disclosure identified below was filed in the Patent and Trademark Office. I hereby request that this Disclosure Document be retained and referenced to the above application.

Disclosure Document Title: ______________________________

Disclosure Document Number: ______________________________

Disclosure Document Filing Date: ______________________________

Very respectfully,

____
Signed Name

______________________________ ______________________________
Date Typed name, Inventor

____
Address

____

Form 12
Class/Subclass Request for PTO Public Search Room

Commissioner of Patents and Trademarks
Attn: Patent Search Division
Washington, DC 20231

Please identify what subject area or Class(es) and subclass(es) cover my idea. My intended invention is described in sketches on the back of this sheet with each part labeled.

My idea has certain features of structure—mode of operation, and intended use, which I have described below.

I understand that there is no charge for this information.

Thank you.

Sincerely,

Name

Address

(1) Features of structure, or how it is constructed

(2) Mode of operation, or how it works

(3) Intended use, or purpose of idea

OVER FOR SKETCHES OF IDEA

(4) Rough sketches of my idea, viewed from all sides with labels to identify each part

OVER FOR LETTER OF EXPLANATION

Form 13
Declaration
Original Application

As below named inventor, I hereby declare that:

My residence, post office address and citizenship are as stated below next to my name; that I verify believe I am the original, first and sole inventor of the invention entitled: ____

____

____

the specification of which is attached hereto.

I hereby state that I have reviewed and understand the contents of the above identified specification, including claims.

I do not know and do not believe that the same was ever known or used in the United States of America before my invention thereof or more than one year prior to this application, that the same was not in public use or on sale in the United States of America thereof, or patented or described in any printed publication in any country before our invention thereof or more than one year prior to this application, that the invention has not been patented or made the subject of an inventor's certificate issued before the date of this application in any country foreign to the United States of America on an application filed by me or my legal representatives or assigns more than twelve months prior to this application, that I acknowledge my duty to disclose information of which I am aware which is material to the examination of this application, and that no application for patent or inventor's certificate on this invention has been filed in any country foreign to the United States of America prior to this application by me or my legal representatives or assigns, except as follows: *none*.

I hereby declare that all statements made herein of my own knowledge are true and that all statements made on information and belief are believed to be true; and further that these statements were made with the knowledge that willful false statements and the like so made are punishable by fine or imprisonment, or both, under Section 1001 of Title 18 of the United States Code and that such willful false statements may jeopardize the validity of the application or any patent issued thereon.

Full Name of Sole Inventor: ____

Inventor's Signature: ____

Date: ____

Residence: ____

Citizenship: ____

Post Office Address: ____

Business Phone #: ____

Form 14
Sample Petition to Revive
in The United States Patent and Trademark Office

Applicant:	)	Examiner:
Serial No:	)	Group Art Unit:
Filed:	)	
For:	)	
	)	
	)	

PETITION TO REVIVE

DATE:

COMMISSIONER OF PATENTS AND TRADEMARKS
ATTN: Office of the Deputy Assistant
Commissioner for Patents
Building 3-11A09
Washington, DC 20231

Sir

Please accept this petition to revive the patent application described above. The abandonment was unintentional. The applicant did not clearly understand that he could not pay the required fee for an extension of the period for response after the expiration of the period of response set in the last Office action. The applicant mailed his response to the last Office action on June 30, 1988, along with a check for $56.00 for an extension of two months. The Examiner in this case indicated that this was not a timely response and hence the application was deemed abandoned.

I have enclosed the petition fee of $28.00 to revive the application.

Sincerely,

Applicant

Address

Form 15
Supplemental Declaration

Applicant: Examiner:

Serial No.: Group Art Unit:

Filed:

For:

Honorable Commissioner of
Patents and Trademarks
Washington, D.C. 20231

ATTENTION: OFFICE OF PUBLICATIONS

I, the undersigned as inventor named in the above application for a Letters Patent, hereby declare that the subject matter of an amendment [filed on], was part of my invention, and was invented before the filing of the original application, above-identified, for such invention; that I have reviewed and understand the contents of the amendment, including the claims; that I do not know and do not believe that the invention was ever known or used in the United States of America before my invention thereof, or was ever patented or described in any printed publication in any country before our invention thereof, or more than one year before said application, or was in public use or on sale in the United States of America more than one year before the date of said application, that said invention has not been patented or made the subject of an inventor's certificate issued before the date of said application in any country foreign to the United States of America on an application filed by me or my legal representatives or assigns more than twelve months prior to said application in the United States of America, and has not been abandoned.

I hereby declare that all statements made herein of my own knowledge are true and that all statements made on information and belief are believed to be true; and further that these statements and the like so made are punishable by fine or imprisonment, or both, under Section 1001 of Title 18 of the United States Code, and that such willful false statements may jeopardize the validity of this application or any patent issuing thereon.

DATE: ______________________________ ______________________________

Inventor

Form 16
Small Entity Verification Statement

Applicant or Patentee:

Serial or Patent No:

Filed or Issued:

Verified Statement (Declaration) Claiming Small Entity Status (37 CFR 1.9 (f) and 1.27 (b)) - Independent Inventor

As a below named inventor, I hereby declare that I qualify as an independent inventor as defined in 37 CFR 1.9(c) for purposes of paying reduced fees under section 41(a) and (b) of Title 35, United States Code, to the Patent and Trademark Office with regard to the invention entitled ____________________ described in

[ ] the specification filed herewith
[ ] application serial no. __________, filed __________
[ ] patent no. _____________, issued ___________

I have not assigned, granted, conveyed or licensed and am under no obligation under contract or law to assign, grant, convey or license, any rights in the invention to any person who could not be classified as an independent inventor under 37 CFR 1.9(d) or a nonprofit organization under 37 CFR 1.9(e).
Each person, concern or organization to which I have assigned, granted, conveyed, licensed or am under an obligation under contract or law to assign, grant, convey or license any rights in the invention is listed below:

[ ] no such person, concern, or organization
[ ] persons, concerns or organizations listed below*
* Separate verified statements are required from each named person, concern or organization having rights to the invention averring to their status as small entities (37 CFR 1.27).

(Continued)

FULL NAME ______________________________

ADDRESS ______________________________

[ ] Individual [ ] Small Business Concern [ ] Nonprofit Organization

FULL NAME ______________________________

ADDRESS ______________________________

[ ] Individual [ ] Small Business Concern [ ] Nonprofit Organization

FULL NAME ______________________________

ADDRESS ______________________________

[ ] Individual [ ] Small Business Concern [ ] Nonprofit Organization

I acknowledge the duty to file, in this application or patent, notification of any change in status resulting in loss of entitlement to small entity status prior to paying, or at the time of paying, the earliest of the issue fee or any maintenance fee due after the date on which status as a small entity is no longer appropriate (37 CFR 1.28(b)).

I hereby declare that all statements made herein of my own knowledge are true and that all statements made on information and belief are believed to be true; and further that these statements were made with the knowledge that willful false statements and the like so made are punishable by fine or imprisonment, or both, under section 1001 of Title 18 of the United States Code, and that such willful false statements may jeopardize the validity of the application, any patent issuing thereon, or any patent to which this verified statement is directed.

____

Name of Inventor Name of Inventor Name of Inventor

____

Signature of Inventor Signature of Inventor Signature of Inventor

____

Date Date Date

Appendix B

Patent and Trademark Office Fees

U.S. PATENT AND TRADEMARK OFFICE

Effective December 16, 1991

The U.S. Patent and Trademark Office has amended its rules of practice in patent and trademark cases. Parts 1 and 2 of Title 37, Code of Federal Regulations to adjust patent and trademark fee amounts.

Any fee payment due and paid on or after December 16, 1991, must be paid in the revised amount. The date of mailing indicated on a proper Certificate of Mailing under either 37 CFR 1.8 or 37 CFR 1.10 will be considered to be the date of receipt and payment in the Office.

As this fee sheet is a summary and the content of rules also may be changing, you should refer to the notice published in the *Federal Register* on December 13, 1991 at 56 FR Part III. See also *Official Gazette* of December 17, 1991.

The fees which are subject to reduction for small entities who have established status (37 CFR 1.27) are shown in a separate column.

For additional information, please contact the PTO Public Service Center at (703) 305-HELP.

PATENT FEES

Fee Code	37 CFR	Description	Fee	Small Entity Fee if applicable
Filing Fees				
101 / 201	1.16(a)	Basic filing fee - utility	690.00	345.00
102 / 202	1.16(b)	Independent claims in excess of three	72.00	36.00
103 / 203	1.16(c)	Claims in excess of twenty	20.00	10.00
104 / 204	1.16(d)	Multiple dependent claim	220.00	110.00
105 / 205	1.16(e)	Surcharge-Late filing fee or oath or declaration	130.00	65.00
106 / 206	1.16(f)	Design filing fee	280.00	140.00
107 / 207	1.16(g)	Plant filing fee	460.00	230.00
108 / 208	1.16(h)	Reissue filing fee	690.00	345.00
109 / 209	1.16(i)	Reissue independent claims over original patent	72.00	36.00
110 / 210	1.16(j)	Reissue claims in excess of 20 and over original patent	20.00	10.00
139	1.17(k)	Non-English specification	130.00	
Extension Fees				
115 / 215	1.17(a)	Extension for response within first month	110.00	55.00
116 / 216	1.17(b)	Extension for response within second month	350.00	175.00
117 / 217	1.17(c)	Extension for response within third month	810.00	405.00
118 / 218	1.17(d)	Extension for response within fourth month	1,280.00	640.00
Appeals/Interference Fees				
119 / 219	1.17(e)	Notice of appeal	260.00	130.00
120 / 220	1.17(f)	Filing a brief in support of an appeal	260.00	130.00
121 / 221	1.17(g)	Request for oral hearing	220.00	110.00
Issue Fees				
142 / 242	1.18(a)	Utility issue fee	1,130.00	565.00
143 / 243	1.18(b)	Design issue fee	400.00	200.00
144 / 244	1.18(c)	Plant issue fee	570.00	285.00
Miscellaneous Fees				
111	1.20(j)	Extension of term of patent	1,000.00	
112	1.17(n)	Requesting publication of SIR - Prior to examiner's action	790.00*	
113	1.17(o)	Requesting publication of SIR - After examiner's action	1,580.00*	
145	1.20(a)	Certificate of correction	70.00	
147	1.20(c)	For filing a request for reexamination	2,180.00	
148 / 248	1.20(d)	Statutory disclaimer	110.00	55.00
Patent Petition Fees				
122		Petitions to the Commissioner, unless otherwise specified	130.00	

PATENT FEES

Fee Code	37 CFR	Description	Fee	Small Entity Fee if applicable
Patent Petition Fees (continued)				
138	1.17(j)	Petition to institute a public use proceeding	1,310.00	
140 / 240	1.17(l)	Petition to revive unavoidably abandoned application	110.00	55.00
141 / 241	1.17(m)	Petition to revive unintentionally abandoned application	1,130.00	565.00
Maintenance Fees:Applications Filed on or after December 12, 1980				
183 / 283	1.20(e)	Due at 3.5 years	900.00	450.00
184 / 284	1.20(f)	Due at 7.5 years	1,810.00	905.00
185 / 285	1.20(g)	Due at 11.5 years	2,730.00	1,365.00
186 / 286	1.20(h)	Surcharge - Late payment within 6 months	130.00	65.00
187	1.20(i)	Surcharge after expiration	600.00	
PCT Fees - National Stage				
154 / 254	1.492(e)	Surcharge - Late filing fee or oath or declaration	130.00	65.00
156	1.492(f)	English translation - after twenty months	130.00	
956 / 957	1.492(a)(1)	IPEA - U.S.	620.00	310.00
958 / 959	1.492(a)(2)	ISA - U.S.	690.00	345.00
960 / 961	1.492(a)(3)	PTO not ISA or IPEA	920.00	460.00
962 / 963	1.492(a)(4)	Claims meet PCT Article 33(1)-(4) - IPEA - U.S.	90.00	45.00
964 / 965	1.492(b)	Claims - extra independent (over three)	72.00	36.00
966 / 967	1.492(c)	Claims - extra total (over twenty)	20.00	10.00
968 / 969	1.492(d)	Claims - multiple dependent	220.00	110.00
970 / 971	1.492(a)(5)	For filing with EPO or JPO search report	800.00	400.00
PCT Fees - International Stage				
150	1.445(a)(1)	Transmittal fee	190.00	
151	1.445(a)(2)	PCT search fee - no U.S. application	600.00†	
152	1.445(a)(3)	Supplemental search per additional invention	160.00†	
153	1.445(a)(2)	PCT search - prior U.S. application	400.00†	
190	1.482(a)(1)	Preliminary examination fee - ISA was the U.S.	440.00†	
191	1.482(a)(1)	Preliminary examination fee - ISA not the U.S.	650.00†	
192	1.482(a)(2)	Additional invention - ISA was the U.S.	140.00†	
193	1.482(a)(2)	Additional invention - ISA not the U.S.	220.00†	

PATENT FEES

Fee Code	37 CFR	Description	Fee	Small Entity Fee if applicable
PCT Fees to WIPO				
800		Basic fee (first thirty pages)	490.00*	
801		Basic supplemental fee (for each page over thirty)	10.00*	
803		Handling fee	150.00*	
803 - 896		Dsignation fee per country	119.00*	
PCT Fee to EPO				
802		International search	1,320.00	
Patent Service Fees				
561	1.19(a)(1)(i)	Printed copy of patent w/o color, regular service	3.00	
562	1.19(a)(1)(ii)	Printed copy of patent w/o color, expedited local service	6.00	
563	1.19(a)(1)(iii)	Printed copy of patent w//o color, ordered via EOS, expedited service	25.00	
564	1.19(a)(2)	Printed copy of plant patent, in color	12.00	
565	1.19(a)(3)	Copy of utility patent or SIR, with color drawings	24.00	
566	1.19(b)(1)(i)	Certified or uncertified copy of patent application as filed, regular service	12.00	
567	1.19(b)(1)(ii)	Certified or uncertified copy of patent application, expedited local service	24.00	
568	1.19(b)(2)	Certified or uncertified copy of patent-related file wrapper and contents	150.00	
569	1.19(b)(3)	Certified or uncertified copy of document, unless otherwise provided	25.00	
570	1.19(b)(4)	For assignment records, abstract of title and certification, per patent	20.00	
571	1.19(c)	Library Service	50.00	
572	1.19(d)	List of U.S. patents and SIRs in subclass	3.00	
573	1.19(e)	Uncertified statement re status of maintenance fee payments	10.00	
574	1.19(f)	Copy of non-U.S. document	12.00	
575	1.19(g)	Comparing and certifying copies, per document, per copy	25.00	
576	1.19(h)	Additional filing receipt, duplicate or corrected due to applicant error	20.00	
577	1.21(c)	Filing a Disclosure Document	10.00	
578	1.21(d)	Local delivery box rental, per annum	50.00	
579	1.21(e)	International type search report	35.00	
580	1.21(g)	Self-service copy charge, per page	0.25	
581	1.21(h)	Recording each patent assignment, agreement or other paper, per property	40.00	
583	1.21(i)	Publication in Official Gazette	20.00	

PATENT FEES

Fee Code	37 CFR	Description	Fee	Small Entity Fee if applicable
Patent Service Fees (continued)				
584	1.21(j)	Labor charges for services, per hour or fraction thereof	30.00	
585	1.21(k)	Unspecified other services	AT COST	
586	1.21(l)	Retaining abandoned application	130.00	
587	1.21(n)	Handling fee for incomplete or improper application	130.00	
588	1.21(o)	Automated Patent System (APS - text) terminal session time, per hour	40.00	
589	1.296	Handling fee for withdrawal of SIR	130.00	
590	1.24	Patent coupons	3.00	
Patent Enrollment Fees				
609	1.21(a)(1)	Admission to examination	290.00	
610	1.21(a)(2)	Registration to practice	100.00	
611	1.21(a)(3)	Reinstatement to practice	15.00	
612	1.21(a)(4)	Copy of certificate of good standing	10.00	
613	1.21(a)(4)	Certificate of good standing - suitable for framing	20.00	
615	1.21(a)(5)	Review of decision of Director, Office of Enrollment and Discipline	120.00	
616	1.21(a)(6)	Regrading of Examination	120.00	

*Reduced by Basic Filing Fee Paid

†Effective December 27, 1991.

*WIPO fees subject to periodic change due to fluctuations in exchange rate. Refer to Patent Official Gazette for current amounts.

TRADEMARK FEES

Fee Code	37 CFR	Description	Fee	Small Entity Fee if applicable
Trademark Processing Fees				
361	2.6(a)(1)	Application for registration, per class	200.00	
362	2.6(a)(2)	Filing an Amendment to Allege Use under § 1(c), per class	100.00	
363	2.6(a)(3)	Filing a Statement of Use under § 1(d)(1), per class	100.00	
364	2.6(a)(4)	Filing a Request for a Six-month Extension of Time for Filing a Statement of Use under § 1(d)(1), per class	100.00	
365	2.6(a)(5)	Application for renewal, per class	300.00	

TRADEMARK FEES

Fee Code	37 CFR	Description	Fee	Small Entity Fee if applicable
Trademark Processing Fees (continued)				
366	2.6(a)(6)	Additional fee for late renewal, per class	100.00	
367	2.6(a)(7)	Publication of mark under §12(c), per class	100.00	
368	2.6(a)(8)	Issuing new certificate of registration	100.00	
369	2.6(a)(9)	Certificate of Correction, registrant's error	100.00	
370	2.6(a)(10)	Filing disclaimer to registration	100.00	
371	2.6(a)(11)	Filing amendment to registration	100.00	
372	2.6(a)(12)	Filing § 8 affidavit, per class	100.00	
373	2.6(a)(13)	Filing §15 affidavit, per class	100.00	
374	2.6(a)(14)	Filing combined §§ 8 & 15 affidavit, per class	200.00	
375	2.6(a)(15)	Petition to the Commissioner	100.00	
376	2.6(a)(16)	Petition for cancellation, per class	200.00	
377	2.6(a)(17)	Notice of opposition, per class	200.00	
378	2.6(a)(18)	Ex parte appeal, per class	100.00	
Trademark Service Fees				
461	2.6(b)(1)(i)	Printed copy of each registered mark, regular service	3.00	
462	2.6(b)(1)(ii)	Printed copy of each registered mark, expedited local service	6.00	
463	2.6(b)(1)(iii)	Printed copy of each registered mark ordered via EOS, expedited service	25.00	
464	2.6(b)(4)(i)	Certified copy of registered mark, with title and/or status, regular service	10.00	
465	2.6(b)(4)(ii)	Certified copy of registered mark, with title and/or status, expedited local service	20.00	
466	2.6(b)(2)(i)	Certified or uncertified copy of trademark application as filed, regular service	12.00	
467	2.6(b)(2)(ii)	Certified or uncertified copy of trademark application as filed, expedited local service	24.00	
468	2.6(b)(3)	Certified or uncertified copy of trademark-related file wrapper and contents	50.00	
469	2.6(b)(5)	Certified or uncertified copy of trademark document, unless otherwise provided	25.00	
470	2.6(b)(7)	For assignment records, abstracts of title and certification per registration	20.00	
475	1.19(g)	Comparing and certifying copies, per document, per copy	25.00	

TRADEMARK FEES

Fee Code	37 CFR	Description	Fee	Small Entity Fee if applicable
Trademark Service Fees (continued)				
480	2.6(b)(9)	Self-service copy charge, per page	0.25	
481	2.6(b)(6)	Recording trademark assignment, agreement or other paper, first mark per document	40.00	
482		For second and subsequent marks on the same document	25.00	
484	2.6(b)(10)	Labor charges for services, per hour or fraction thereof	30.00	
485	2.6(b)(11)	Unspecified other services	AT COST	
488	2.6(b)(8)	Each hour of T-SEARCH terminal session time	40.00	
490	1.24	Trademark coupons	3.00	

GENERAL FEES

Fee Code	37 CFR	Description	Fee	Small Entity Fee if applicable
Finance Service Fees				
607	1.21(b-1)	Establish a deposit account	10.00	
608	1.21(b)(2)	Service charge for below minimum balance	20.00	
608	1.21(b)(3)	Service charge for below minimum balance restricted subscription deposit account	20.00	
617	1.21(m)	Processing returned checks	50.00	
Computer Service Fees				
618		Computer records	AT COST	

Appendix C

Select Bibliography

Amernick, Burton A. *Patent Law for the Nonlawyer: A Guide for the Engineer, Technologist and Manager*. 2nd ed. New York: Van Nostrand Reinhold, 1991.

Arnold, T., and Vaden, Frank S., III. *Invention Protection for Practicing Engineers*. New York: Barnes and Noble, 1971.

Berle, Alf Keyser. *Inventions and Their Management*, 1st ed. Scranton, PA: International Textbook Company, 1937.

Biesterfield, Chester H. *Patent Law for Lawyers, Students, Chemists and Engineers*. New York: John Wiley & Sons, Inc., London: Chapman and Hall, 1949.

Calvert, Robert, Eg. *The Encyclopedia of Patent Practice and Invention Management*. New York: Reinhold Publishing Corp., 1964.

Carter, E. F. *Dictionary of Inventions and Discoveries*, 2nd rev. ed. New York: Crane Russak, 1976.

Code of Federal Regulations, Title 37-Patents, Trademarks, and Copyrights. Revised annually. U.S. Government Printing Office. Available from the Superintendent of Documents, Washington, DC 20402.

Cropp, J., Harris, D., and Stern, E. *Trade in Innovation-The Ins and Outs of Licensing*. New York: Reinhold Publishing Corp., 1964.

DeForest, Thomas E. *Inventor's Guide to Successful Patent Applications*, 1st ed. Blue Ridge Summit, PA: Tab Books, 1988.

DeGarmo, E. P. *Engineering Economy, 4th ed*. New York: The Macmillan Co., 1967.

DeSimone, D. V. *Education for Innovation*. Elsmford, NY: Pergamon Press, 1968.

Doi, T., and Shattuck, W. *Patent and Know-How Licensing in Japan and the United States*, No. 5. Seattle, WA: University of Washington Press, 1977.

Do You Know Your Economic ABC's? Patents: Spur to American Progress. Washington, DC: U.S. Government Printing Office, 1969.

Dummer, G. W. A. *Electronic Inventions and Discoveries*, 2nd ed. Oxford, England: Pergamon Press, 1978.

Einhorn, Harold. *Patent Licensing Transactions*. New York: Matthew Bender, 1977.

Finnegan, Marcus B., and Goldscheider, Robert. *The Law and Business of Licensing.* New York: Clark Boardman Co., 1977.

Foltz, Ramon D. *Protecting Scientific Ideas and Inventions.* Boca Raton, FL: CRC Press, 1988.

General Information Concerning Patents. Washington, DC: U.S. Department of Commerce, 1974.

Gilmore, F. E. *How to Invent, A Guide to the Mental Techniques of Learning to Invent and Their Application to Your Daily Thinking.* Houston, TX: Gulf Publishing Co., 1959.

Grant, E. L. and Ireson, W. G., *Principles of Engineering Economy.* 5th ed. New York: The Ronald Press Co., 1970.

Greene, Orville. *The Practical Inventor's Handbook.* New York: McGraw-Hill, 1979.

Guide for Patent Draftsmen. U.S. Government Printing Office. Available from the Superintendent of Documents, Washington, DC 20402.

Hoff, Paul S. *Inventions in the Marketplace: Patent Licensing and the U.S. Antitrust Laws.* Washington, DC: American Enterprise Institute for Public Policy Research, 1986.

Index to the U. S. Patent Classification. U.S. Patent and Trademark Office. Available at all patent depository libraries.

Jones, Stacy V. *The Inventor's Patent Handbook.* New York: Dial Press, 1966.

Kintner, Early W., and Lahr, Jack L. *An Intellectual Property Law Primer.* New York: The Macmillan Co., 1975.

Kivenson, G. *The Art and Science of Inventing.* New York: Van Nostrand Reinhold, 1977.

Klooster, John W. *The Granting of Inventive Rights.* Minneapolis, MN: Intel-Lex, 1965.

Kock, W. E. *The Creative Engineer, The Art of Inventing.* New York: Plenum Press, 1978.

Levy, Richard C. *Inventing and Patenting Sourcebook: How to Sell and Protect Your Ideas,* 1st ed. Detroit, MI: Gale Research, 1990.

Licensing Guide for Developing Countries. Geneva, Switzerland: World Intellectual Property Organization, Section des Publications, 32 Chemin des Columbettes, 1211 Geneva 20, Switzerland, 1977.

MacCracken, Calvin D. *A Handbook for Inventors: How to Protect, Patent, Finance, Develop, Manufacture, and Market Your Ideas.* New York: Scribner's, 1983.

Manual of Patent Classification. U.S. Patent and Trademark Office. Available at all patent depository libraries.

Manual of Patent Examining Procedure. U.S. Government Printing Office. Available from the Superintendent of Documents, Washington, DC 20402.

Mayers, Harry R. *Drafting Patent License Agreements with Related Treatment of Know-How Transactions.* Washington, DC: The Bureau of National Affairs, 1971.

McNair, E. P. and Schwenck, J. E. *How to Become a Successful Inventor.* New York: Hastings House, 1973.

Miller, P. Q. *Everything You Always Wanted to Know about Inventing, an Annotated and Selected Bibliography.* Washington, DC: U.S. Patent Office Scientific Library, 1974.

Nordhaus, Raymond, C. *Patent License Agreements (Law and Forms)*. Chicago, IL: Jural Publishing Company, 1977.

Official Gazette of the U.S. Patent and Trademark Office. U.S. Government Printing Office. Available at all patent depository libraries.

Patent Classification Definitions. U.S. Patent and Trademark Office. Available at all patent depository libraries.

Patent Laws. U.S. Patent and Trademark Office. Washington, DC: U.S. Government Printing Office.

.Pressman, David. *Patent It Yourself!: How to Protect, Patent, and Market Your Inventions*. New York: McGraw-Hill, 1979.

Prostano, Emanuel T. *Educators Guide to Patents and Inventions*. New Haven, CT: In-Time Publications, 1990.

Questions and Answers About Patents: Answers to Questions Frequently Asked About Patents. Washington, DC: U.S. Patent and Trademark Office.

Rawy, W. and Ray, M. *The Art of Invention, Patent Models and Their Markers*. Princeton, NJ: Pyne Press, 1974.

Rivkin, Bernard. *Patenting and Marketing Your Invention*. New York: Van Nostrand Reinhold, 1986.

Rosenberg, Peter D. *Patent Law Fundamentals*. New York: Clark Boardman Co., 1975.

Sanderson, William R. *Patent Your Invention and Make it Pay*. New York: Grosset & Dunlap, 1966.

Shlesinger, B. E. Jr. *The Art of Successful Inventing*. Arlington, VA: Hafner Publications, 1974.

Sperber, Philip. *Intellectual Property Management: Law-Business-Strategy*, Vol. 3. New York: Clark Boardman Co., 1974.

The ABC's of Intellectual Property. Washington, DC: Intellectual Property Owners, Inc.

Trademark Licensing. New York: The United States Trademark Association, 1962.

Tuska, Clarence D. *An Introduction to Patents for Inventors and Engineers*. New York: Dover Publications, 1964.

White, R. S. *Patent Litigation, Procedures and Tactics*. New York: Matthew Bender, 1974.

Winfield, Armand G. *The Inventor's Handbook*. Englewood Cliffs, NJ: Prentice Hall, 1990.

Wright, Everett Gardiner. *Patents: A Concise Informative Guide to Patents for Executives, Engineers, Attorneys and Inventors*. Detroit, MI: Patents Pub. Co., 1934.

SBA Directory of Business Development Publications

Financial Management and Analysis

FM1	*ABCs of Borrowing* Some small business people cannot understand why a lending institution refused to lend them money. Others have no trouble getting funds but are surprised to find strings attached to their loans. Learn the fundamentals of borrowing.	$1.00
FM2	*Profit Costing and Pricing for Manufacturers* Uncover the latest techniques for pricing your products profitably.	$1.00
FM3	*Basic Budgets for Profit Planning* This publication takes the worry out of putting together a comprehensive budgeting system to monitor your profits and assess your financial operations.	$0.50
FM4	*Understanding Cash Flow* In order to survive, a business must have enough cash to meet its obligations. The owner/manager is shown how to plan for the movement of cash through the business and thus plan for future requirements.	
FM5	*A Venture Capital Primer for Small Business* This best-seller highlights the venture capital resources available and how to develop a proposal for obtaining these funds.	$0.50
FM6	*Accounting Services for Small Business Firms* Sample profit/loss statements are used to illustrate how accounting services can help expose and correct trouble spots in a business' financial records.	$0.50
FM7	*Analyze Your Records and Reduce Costs* Cost reduction is not simply slashing any and all expenses. Understand the nature of expenses and how they inter-relate with sales, inventories, and profits. Achieve greater profits through more efficient use of the dollar.	$0.50
FM8	*Budgeting in a Small Firm* Learn how to set up and keep sound financial records. Study how to effectively use journals, ledgers and charts to increase profits.	$0.50
FM9	*Sound Cash Management and Borrowing* Avoid a "cash crisis" through proper use of cash budgets, cash flow projections, and planned borrowing concepts.	$0.50
FM10	*Recordkeeping in a Small Business* Need some basic advice on setting up a useful record keeping system? This publication describes how.	$1.00
FM11	*Simple Breakeven Analysis for Small Stores* Learn how "breakeven analysis" enables the manager/owner to make better decisions concerning sales, profits, and costs.	$1.00
FM12	*A Pricing Checklist for Small Retailers* The owner/manager of a small retail business can use this checklist to apply proven pricing strategies that can lead to profits.	$0.50
FM13	*Pricing Your Products and Services Profitably* Discusses how to price your products profitably, how to use the various techniques of pricing, and when to use these techniques to your advantage.	$1.00

General Management and Planning

MP1	*Effective Business Communications* Explains the importance of business communications and how they play a valuable role in business success.	$0.50

General Management and Planning *(continued)*

MP2	*Locating or Relocating Your Business* Learn how a company's market, available labor force, transportation, and raw materials are affected when selecting a business location.	$1.00
MP3	*Problems in Managing a Family-Owned Business* Specific problems exist when attempting to make a family-owned business successful. This publication offers suggestions on how to overcome these difficulties.	$0.50
MP4	*Business Plan for Small Manufacturers* Designed to help an owner/manager of a small manufacturing firm. This publication covers all the basic information necessary to develop an effective business plan.	$1.00
MP5	*Business Plan for Small Construction Firms* This publication is designed to help an owner/manager of a small construction company pull together the resources to develop a business plan.	$1.00
MP6	*Planning and Goal Setting for Small Business* Learn how to plan for success.	$0.50
MP7	*Fixing Production Mistakes* Structured as a checklist, this publication emphasizes the steps that should be taken by a manufacturer when a production mistake has been found.	$0.50
MP8	*Should You Lease or Buy Equipment?* Describes various aspects of the lease/buy decision. It lists advantages and disadvantages of leasing and provides a format for comparing the costs of the two.	$0.50
MP9	*Business Plan for Retailers* Learn how to develop a business plan for a retail business.	$1.00
MP10	*Choosing a Retail Location* Learn about current retail site selection techniques such as demographic and traffic analysis. This publication addresses the hard questions the retailer must answer before making the choice of a store location.	$1.00
MP11	*Business Plan for Small Service Firms* Outlines the key points to be included in the business plan of a small service firm.	$0.50
MP12	*Checklist for Going Into Business* This best-seller highlights important considerations you should know in reaching a decision to start your own business. It also includes a checklist for going into business.	$0.50
MP14	*How to Get Started with a Small Business Computer* Helps you forecast your computer needs, evaluate the alternative choices, and select the right computer system for your business.	$1.00
MP15	*The Business Plan for Homebased Business* Provides a comprehensive approach to developing a business plan for a homebased business. If you are convinced that a profitable home business is attainable, this publication will provide a step-by-step guide to develop a plan for your business.	$1.00
MP16	*How to Buy or Sell a Business* Learn several techniques used in determining the best price to buy or sell a small business.	$1.00
MP17	*Purchasing for Owners of Small Plants* Presents an outline of an effective purchasing program. Also includes a bibliography for further research into industrial purchasing.	$0.50

General Management and Planning *(continued)*

MP18	*Buying for Retail Stores* Discusses the latest trends in retail buying. Includes a bibliography that references a wide variety of private and public sources of information on most aspects of retail buying.	$1.00
MP19	*Small Business Decision Making* Acquaint yourself with the wealth of information available on management approaches to identify, analyze and solve business problems.	$1.00
MP20	*Business Continuation Planning* Provides an overview of business owner's life insurance needs that are not typically considered until after the death of one of the business' principal owners.	$1.00
MP21	*Developing a Strategic Business Plan* Helps you develop a strategic action plan for your small business.	$1.00
MP22	*Inventory Management* Discusses the purpose of inventory management, types of inventories, record keeping and forecasting inventory levels.	$0.50
MP23	*Techniques for Problem Solving* Instructs the small business person on the key techniques of problem solving and problem identification, as well as designing and implementing a plan to correct these problems.	$1.00
MP24	*Techniques for Productivity Improvement* Learn to increase worker output through motivating "quality of work life" concepts and tailoring benefits to meet the needs of the employees.	$1.00
MP25	*Selecting the Legal Structure for Your Business* Discusses the various legal structures that a small business can use in setting up its operations. It briefly identifies the types of legal structures and lists the advantages and disadvantages of each.	$0.50
MP26	*Evaluating Franchise Opportunities* Although the success rate for franchise-owned businesses is significantly better than start-up businesses, success is not guaranteed. Evaluate franchise opportunities and select the business that's right for you.	$0.50
MP27	*Starting a Retail Travel Agency* Travel agencies are a rewarding yet challenging business. Learn how to start your own agency.	$1.00
MP28	*Small Business Risk Management Guide* Strengthen your insurance program by identifying, minimizing and eliminating business risks. This guide can help you secure adequate insurance protection for your company.	$1.00
MP29	*Quality Child Care Makes Good Business Sense* Starting a childcare center involves all the challenges of any small business and also requires dedication to the well being of the children. This comprehensive manual, developed by childcare professionals in both private and public sectors, explains the business and academic dimensions of operating a childcare center.	$2.00

Marketing

MT1	*Creative Selling: Competitive Edge* Explains how to use creative selling techniques to increase profits.	$0.50

Marketing *(continued)*

MT2	*Marketing for Small Business: An Overview* Provides an overview of "Marketing" concepts and contains an extensive bibliography of sources covering the subject of marketing.	$1.00
MT3	*Is the Independent Sales Agent For You?* Provides guidelines that help the owner of a small company determine if a sales agent is needed and pointers on how to choose one.	$0.50
MT4	*Marketing Checklist for Small Retailers* This checklist is for the owner/manager of a small retail business. The questions outlined cover customer analysis, buying, pricing, and promotion and other factors in the retail marketing process.	$1.00
MT8	*Researching Your Market* Learn what market research is and how you can benefit from it. Introduces inexpensive techniques that small business owners can apply to gather facts about their customer base and how to expand it.	$1.00
MT9	*Selling by Mail Order* Provides basic information on how to run a successful mail order business. Includes information on product selection, pricing, testing, and writing effective advertisements.	$1.00
MT10	*Market Overseas with U.S. Government Help* Entering the overseas marketplace offers exciting opportunities to increase company sales and profits. Learn about the programs available to help small business break into the world of exporting.	$1.00
MT11	*Advertising* Advertising is critical to the success of any small business. Learn how you can effectively market your products and services.	$1.00

Personnel Management

PM1	*Checklist for Developing a Training Program* Describes a step-by-step process of setting up an effective employee training program.	$0.50
PM2	*Employees: How to Find and Pay Them* A business is only as good as the people in it. Learn how to find and hire the right employees.	$1.00
PM3	*Managing Employee Benefits* Describes employee benefits as one part of the total compensation package and discusses proper management of benefits.	$1.00

New Products/Ideas/Inventions

PI1	*Can You Make Money with Your Idea or Invention?* This publication is a step-by-step guide which shows how you can make money by turning your creative ideas into marketable products. It is a resource for entrepreneurs attempting to establish themselves in the marketplace.	$0.50
PI2	*Introduction to Patents* Offers some basic facts about patents to help clarify your rights. It discusses the relationships among a business, an inventor, and the Patent and Trademark Office to ensure protection of your product and to avoid or win infringement suits.	$0.50

To order Small Business Administration publication, follow these steps.

1. Write down the publication number and title and how many you want, if more than one.
2. Include the total number of publications you've ordered, and the total dollar amount enclosed.
3. Make your check or money order payable to:
   U.S. Small Business Administration
   (Note: No cash, credit cards, or purchase orders!)
4. Be sure to include your name, address, city, and state, and zip code.
5. Mail all this information with your donation to:
   SBA-Publications
   P.O. Box 30
   Denver, Colorado 80201-0030

Appendix D

Selected Rules of Practice Relating to Patent Drawings

GUIDE FOR PATENT DRAWINGS

An applicant for a patent is required to furnish a drawing of his or her invention whenever the nature of the invention permits it; the drawing must be filed with the application. Illustrations facilitating the understanding of the invention may also be furnished in the same manner as drawings. These illustrations may be in the forms of flow sheets in cases of processes and diagramatic views. Drawing is herein meant to convey one of several figures or views.

The content of drawings should be as follows:

- The drawings must show every feature of the invention specified in the claims. However, conventional features disclosed in the description and claims, where their detailed illustration is not essential for a proper understanding of the invention, should be illustrated in the drawing in the form of a graphic symbol or a labeled representation (e.g., a labeled rectangular box).
- When the invention consists of an improvment on an old machine, the drawing must when possible exhibit, in one or more views, the improved portion itself, disconnected from the old structure; and in another view, only so much of the old structure as suffices to show the connection with the invention.
- The drawing(s) should be planned so that one of the views will be representative and suitable for publication in the *Official Gazette* and on the title page of the patent as the illustration of the invention.

SYMBOLS AND LEGENDS FOR MECHANICAL AND ELECTRICAL DEVICES

Graphic symbols and labeled representations (Figures D-1 and D-2) may be used for conventional elements when appropriate, subject to approval by the office. The elements for which they are used must be adequately identified in the specification. Suitable legends may be used, or may be required in proper cases, as in diagrammatic views and flow sheets or to show materials (Figure D-8) where labeled representations are employed to illustrate conventional elements.

The lettering should be as large as, or larger than, the reference characters. Arrows may be used to show direction of movement.

LETTERS AND FIGURES OF REFERENCE

Letters and figures of reference must be carefully formed. See Figure D-3. Several types of lettering and figure marks are shown; however, the draftsman may use any style of lettering that he or she chooses.

EDGE SHADING

Place heavy lines on the shaded side of objects, assuming that the light is coming from the upper left-hand corner at an angle of 45 degrees. Make these heavy lines the same weight throughout the various views on the drawing, as shown in Figure D-4.

SURFACE SHADING

Surface delineations should be shown by proper shading. Figure D-5 shows various types of surface shading. The amount of shading necessary depends on the size of the diameter of the shaft, etc. Note that a single heavy line on the shadow side is sufficient shading for small pipes, rods, and shafts. When more than one shaded line is used on cylindrical surfaces, the shading is blended from the second line. Note that the outer line is a light line. This rule on shading applies to spherical as well as cylindrical surfaces.

PERSPECTIVES

The three examples in Figure D-6 in perspective clearly explain the fundamental rules for determining the position of the long axis of the ellipse. Do not add the center lines, as they are not permitted on patent drawings. These have been shown for instructive purposes only.

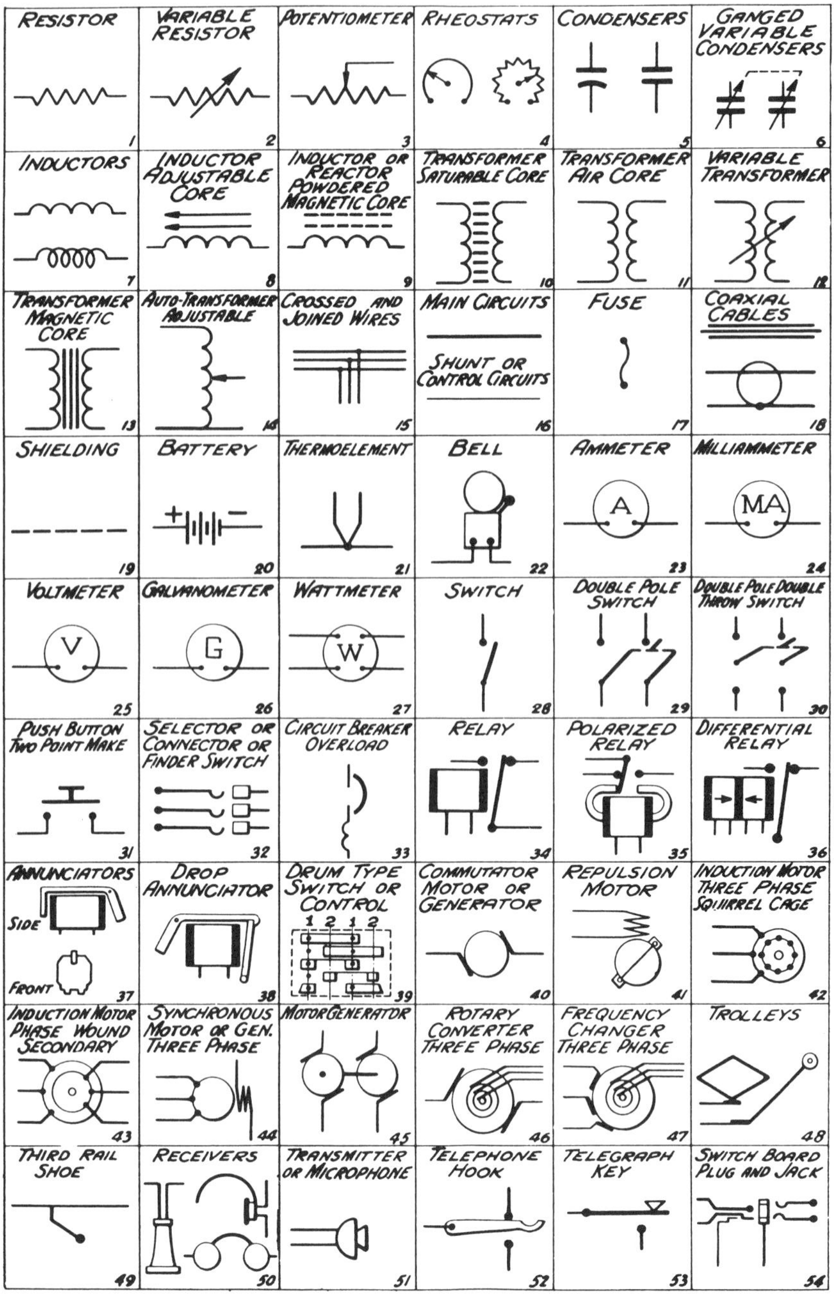

FIGURE D-1. Electrical Symbols

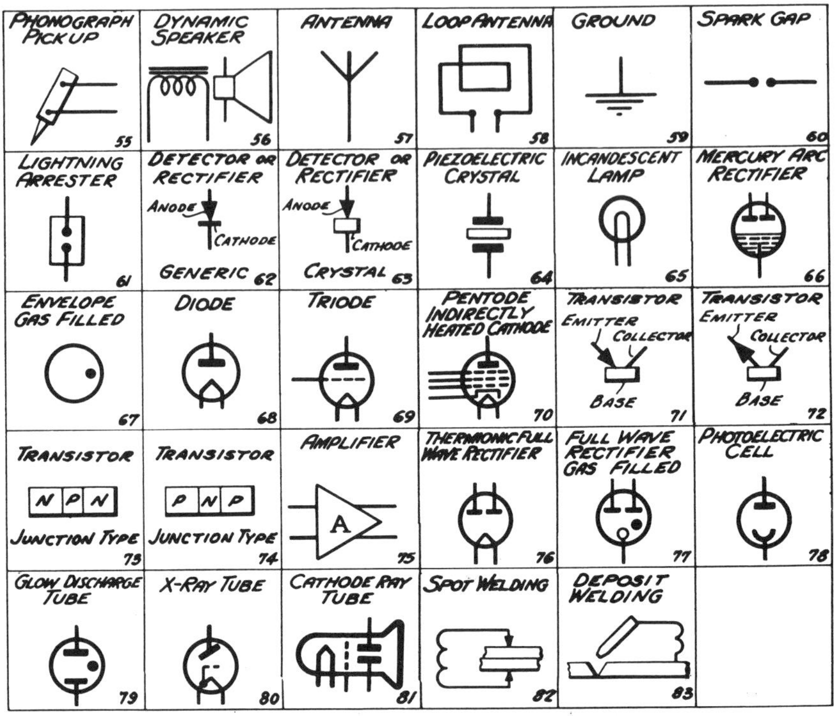

FIGURE D-1. *(continued)*

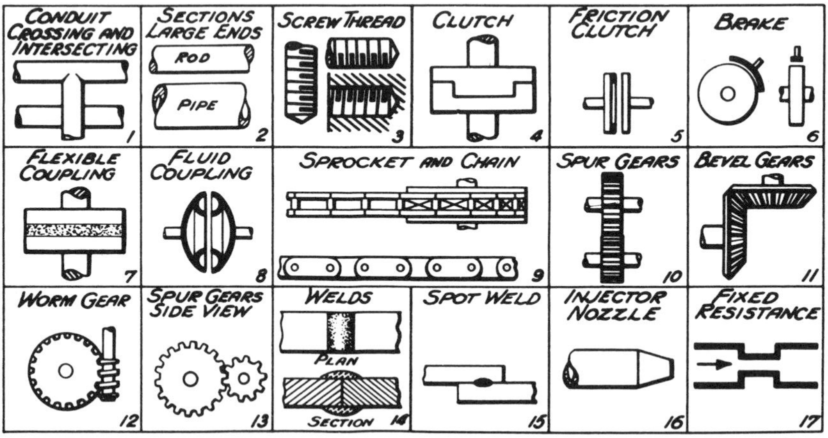

FIGURE D-2. Mechanical Symbols

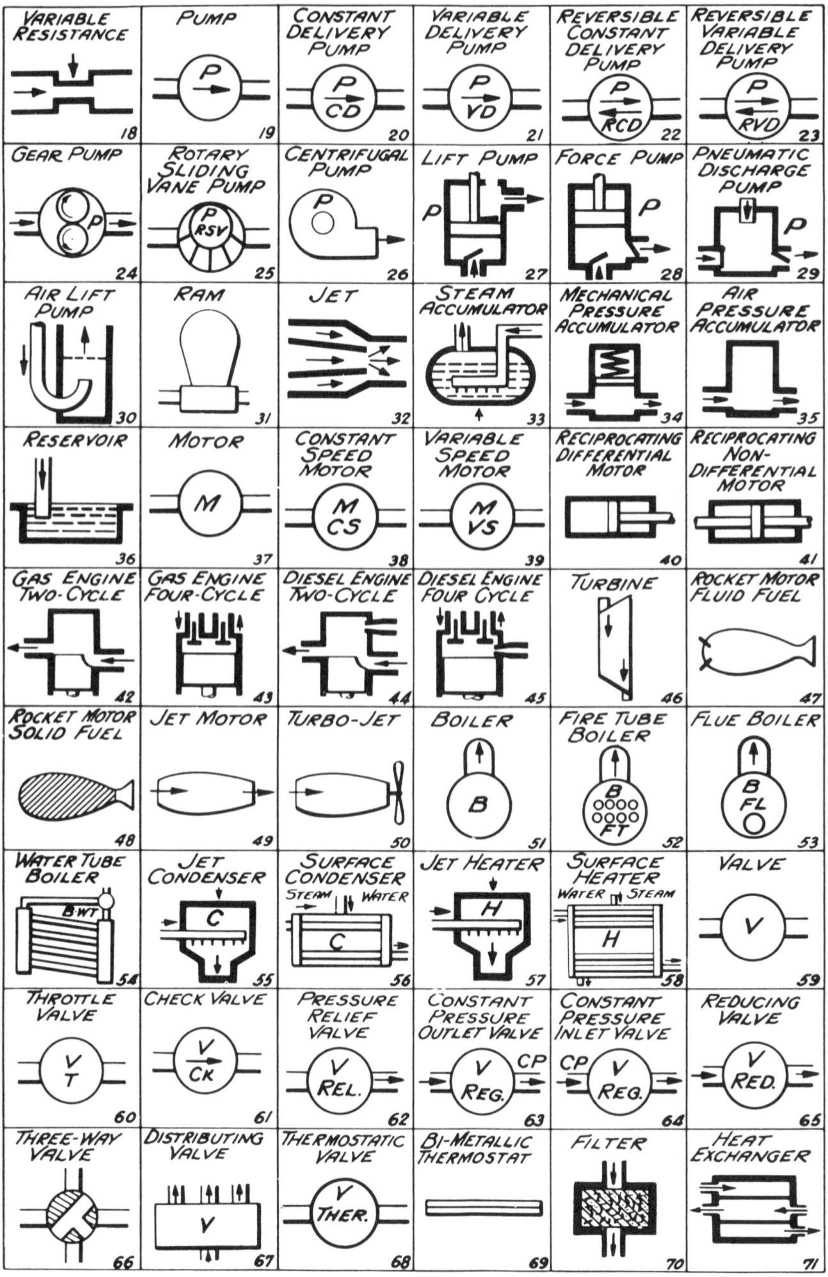

FIGURE D-2. *(continued)*

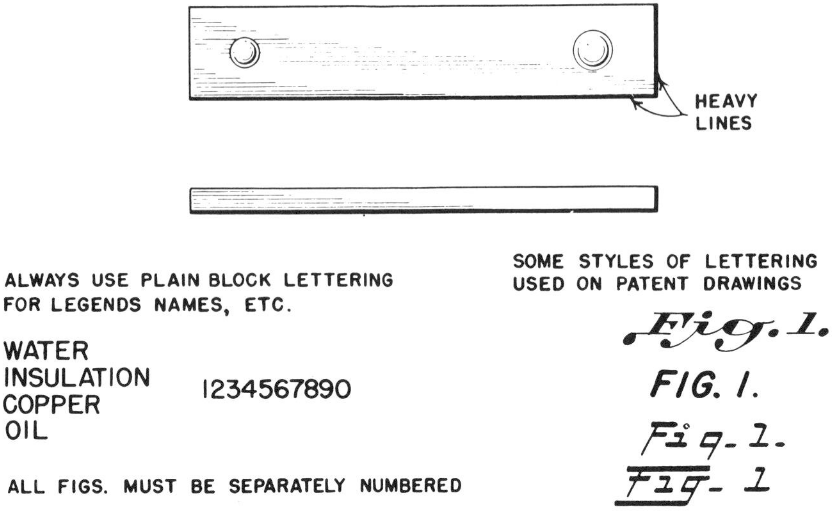

FIGURE D-3. Letters and Figures of Reference

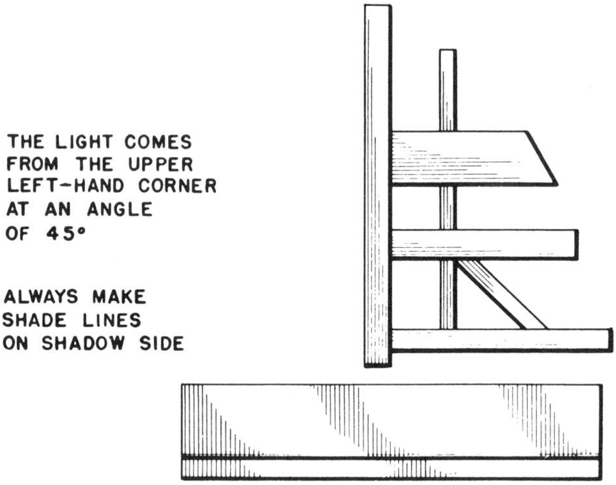

FIGURE D-4. Position of Heavy Lines on Objects

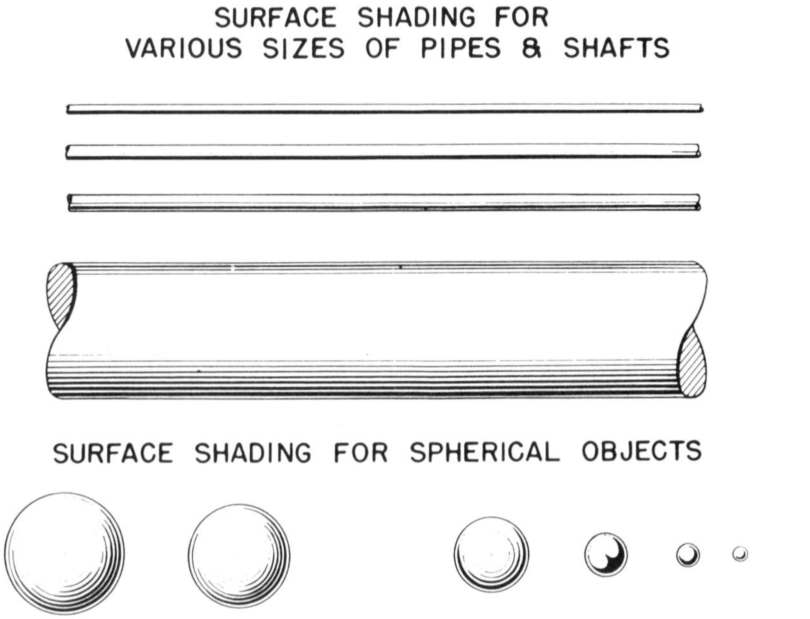

FIGURE D-5. Surface Shading

REFERENCE CHARACTERS

Reference characters should be placed as close as possible to parts to which they refer (Figure D-7). They should be connected with these parts by a short lead line, never by a long lead line. When necessary, blank spaces must be left unshaded and hatched areas used for applying the numerals.

MATERIAL IDENTIFICATION SYMBOLS

Material identification symbols are given in Figure D-8.

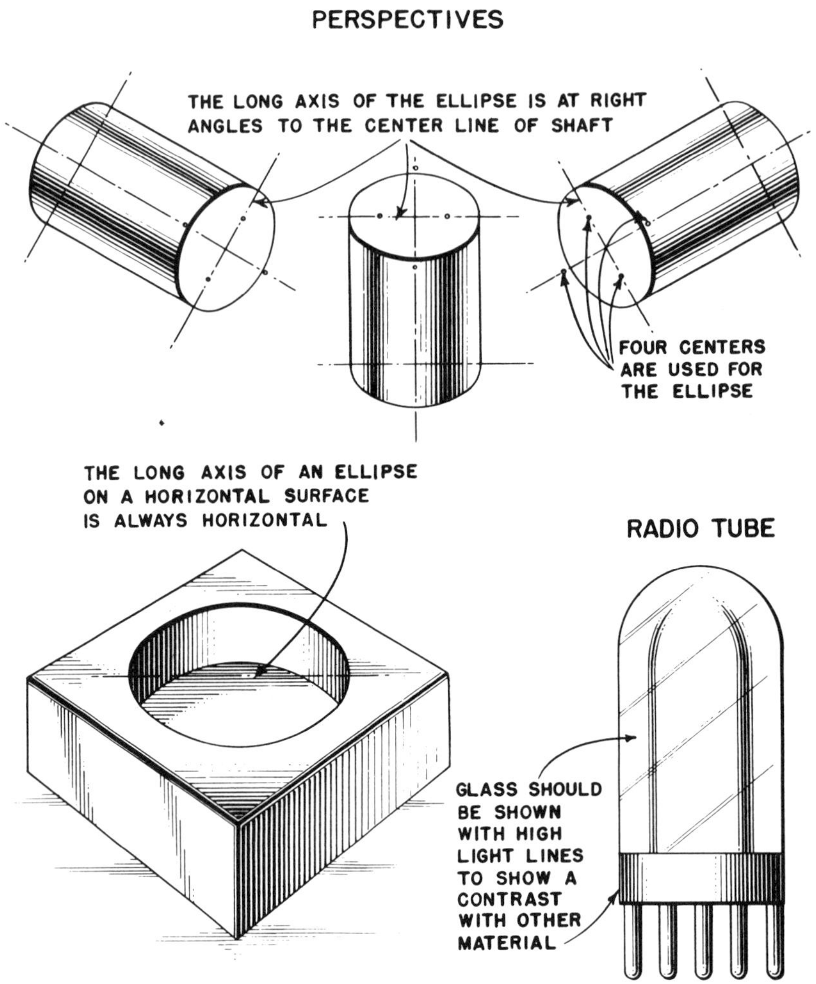

FIGURE D-6. Perspective Views

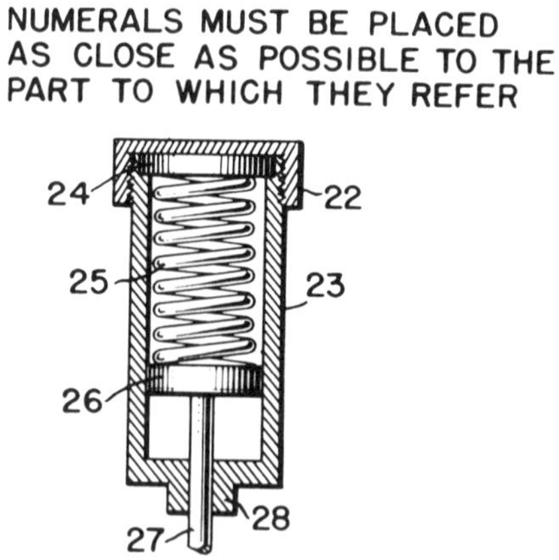

FIGURE D-7. Numbering of Component Parts

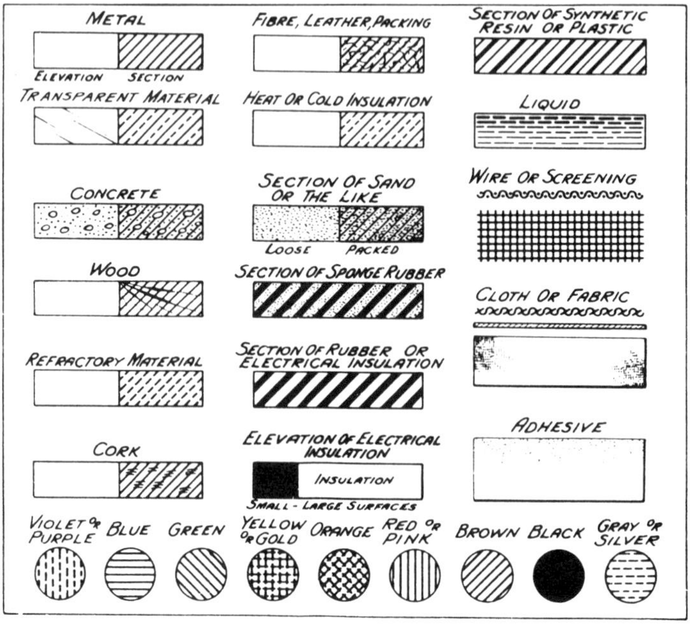

FIGURE D-8. Material Identification

Appendix E

Patent Copies

Sept. 1, 1931. I. H. FOTHERINGHAM 1,821,627

TYPE OF ARTICULATED AND DISMOUNTABLE LIFTING JACK

Filed Feb. 14, 1929

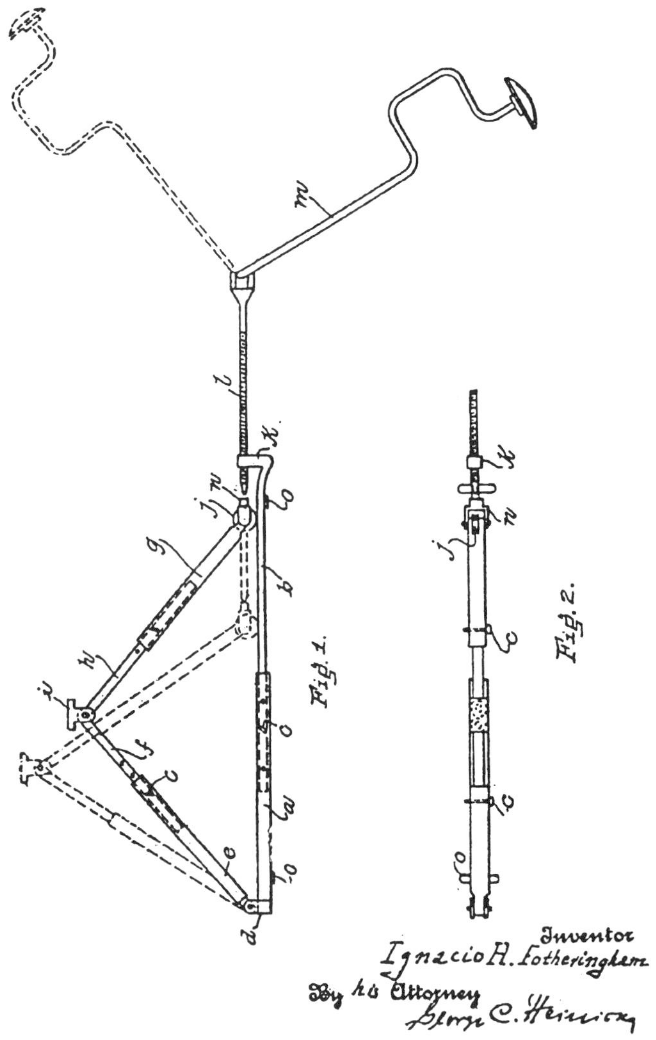

UNITED STATES PATENT OFFICE

1,821,627

Patented Sept. 1, 1931

IGNACIO H. FOTHERINGHAM, OF RIO CUARTO, ARGENTINA

TYPE OF ARTICULATED AND DISMOUNTABLE LIFTING JACK

Application filed February 14, 1929. Serial No. 339,807.

The present invention refers to a new type of articulated and dismountable lifting jack, with the use of which notable advantages are secured, inasmuch as I obtain an appliance of low cost, easy to assemble and dismount, and therefore, very convenient as regards transport and conservation, it being especially adaptable for these reasons for lifting motor cars and similar vehicles, as the reduced space which it occupies, allows it to be carried in any position.

In order that my application may be more comprehensible, I have illustrated same with various figures, wherein:

Fig. 1 is a front view of the apparatus,
Fig. 2 is a plan view.

Construction

The construction comprises essentially an articulated triangle, the base being formed by a pipe or tube (a), in which is inserted the stem (b) for the purpose of its greater or lesser lengthening, fixed by the key (c) which is placed in the holes possessed by the pipe (a) and the stem (b). The pipe (a) has in its end a double ear or lug (d) in which another side of the triangle mentioned moves articulately, and which is constituted by a tube or pipe (e) and the stem (f) which is inserted in same.

The other side of the triangle is also formed by a pipe (g) and its stem (h), fixed in the same manner as the base, that is to say, by its corresponding key and holes, and it is articulated at the vertex, at which is pivoted the support (i).

The pipe *g* is provided at its lower end with a forked member *n* attached thereto by means of a pin carrying between the prongs of the forked member a wheel *j* adapted to run on stem *b* and tube *a* forming the base of the instrument, and stem *b* is equipped at its outer end with a perforated upright part *k* through the perforation of which passes one end of a screw *l*, the other end of which is forked and has articulated thereto a lever *m*, the outer end of which is looped to present a handle.

The base (a),(b) carries the supports (o).

The material with which the distinct parts of the present appliance will be manufactured, may be any adaptable to the various functions to be performed. Also the sides which form the triangle already specified may be of one sole piece, or more if same be necessary, without this representing a departure from the scope of the invention.

Working

Once the triangle has been fixed in the position shown in Fig. 1, in the right hand end of screw (l) is inserted the bi-articulated handle (m), and the screw (l) is placed in movement. This screw (l), pushes the fork (n), which in turn pushes pertaining side, whose wheel (j) slides upon the base (b), (a) of the triangle, modifying the figure of this and raising the vertex (i), (also articulated), thus raising the object resting on the vertex mentioned, as shown by dotted lines in Fig. 1.

The greater or lesser length of the sides is easily obtained by means of the insertion indicated, and by the keys and holes already explained.

The load or object having been raised, and it being desired to lower same, it is sufficient to reverse the movement of the handle (m) in order to effect the descent, smoothly and securely, avoiding violent descents through failure of parts or carelessness, these inconveniences being completely eliminated with the present appliance.

Having thus described my invention what I claim as new and desire to secure by Letter Patent is:

A lifting jack comprising an extensible base, an extensible arm pivoted to said base and extending upwardly at an inclination thereto, a second extensible arm pivoted to the upper end of the first extensible arm and extending downwardly at an inclination from said second pivot, said second named arm having a roller connected to its lower end to travel on the base, a support connected to the last mentioned pivot, a perforated upright secured to one end of the base, a screw threaded through the perforation of said upright, a handle pivotally connected to the screw, a member connected to the lower end of the second named arm and extending towards and adapted to engage the free end of the screw whereby upon rotation of the screw by the handle the member will move the roller over the bar to thereby elevate the arms and the support.

In testimony whereof I affix my signature

IGNACIO H. FOTHERINGHAM

April 10, 1962 C. BUDDINGH 3,029,065

MEANS FOR MOVING VEHICLES 2,672

Filed Jan. 15, 1960

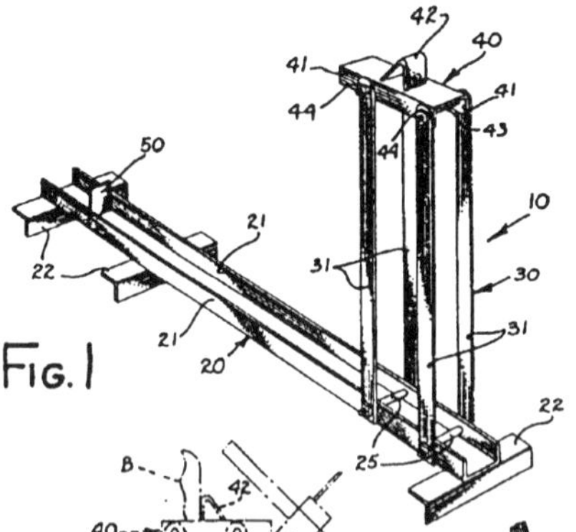

FIG. 1

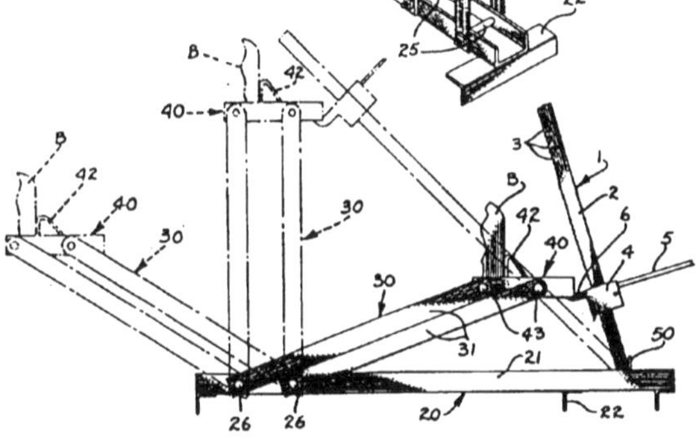

FIG. 2

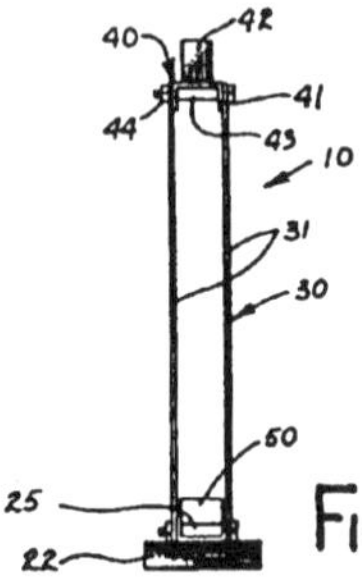

FIG. 3

INVENTOR
CORNELIUS BUDDINGH

BY Price and Heneveld

ATTORNEYS

UNITED STATES PATENT OFFICE 3,029,065

Patented Apr.10,1962

CORNELIUS BUDDINGH, CALEDONIA, MICH.

MEANS FOR MOVING VEHICLES

Filed Jan. 15, 1960, Ser. No. 2,672
8 Claims. (Cl. 254—35)

This invention relates to a means for moving vehicles. More particularly, this invention relates to an apparatus for moving a vehicle out of a hole and the like, the apparatus adapted to be used in combination with an ordinary bumper jack.

Many times, the operator of an automobile finds himself unable to move the car out of a hole or rut caused by mud, snow, etc. Most of the time, the rear tires of the automobile are positioned in the hole or rut such that if a means could be provided to move the automobile a foot or two in either direction, the automobile would no longer be immovable under its own power. Bumper jacks presently in existence are merely adapted to raise or lower an automobile so that they provide little help in such a situation. Consequently, the driver must have his automobile towed out of the rut. This is especially true in the case of automobiles having automatic transmissions since the drive cannot "rock" the automobile back and forth in attempting to get out of such a rut.

It is an object of this invention to provide an apparatus which is especially adapted for moving an automobile up out of such a rut and a foot or two forward away from the rut. This apparatus is adapted to be used in combination with an ordinary bumper jack of the type which is considered standard equipment in automobile trunks.

Another object of this invention is to provide such an apparatus which is compact enough so that it may be carried in the trunk of an automobile at all times.

Another object of this invention is to provide such an apparatus which operates in such a manner so that it performs the hereinbefore described function safely, quickly, and simply.

A still further object of this invention is to provide such an apparatus using a minimum of parts, making it inexpensive enough to be a practical item for all automobile owners.

These and other objects of this invention will become obvious to those skilled in the art relating to such equipment upon reading the following specification in conjunction with the accompanying drawings, wherein:

FIG. 1 is a perspective view of the apparatus comprising this invention;

FIG. 2 is a side, elevational view of the apparatus shown in FIG. 1, the various positions of the apparatus during operation being shown in dotted lines; and

FIG. 3 is an end view of the apparatus shown in FIG. 1.

The apparatus comprising this invention is adapted to be used in combination with a bumper jack of standard construction. Such a bumper jack is shown in FIG. 2 and is designated by the reference numeral 1. The bumper jack 1 includes an upstanding bar 2 having a plurality of notches 3 on one surface thereof. The member 4 slidably envelopes the bar 2, the member 4 riding up the bar 2 on the notches 3 by means of movement of the handle 5. The outwardly projecting finger 6 is adapted to ordinarily be positioned under the bumper of an automobile, thereby raising the automobile as the member 4 is moved up the bar 2. Such a bumper jack does not comprise a part of this invention, but rather is shown and described since the apparatus comprising the invention may be used in combination therewith.

The apparatus for moving a vehicle for use in combination with such a bumper jack comprises a ground engaging member having an elongated arm member pivotally connected thereto. Means is provided on the free end of this elongated member for bearing against and supporting a vehicle. Means are also provided on the ground engaging member and the elongated arm member for receiving a bumper jack whereby the elongated member may be pivoted about its pivotal connection. As the elongated member thus pivots, the vehicle is first raised and then moved forward to be again lowered at a point away from its original position.

Turning specifically to the drawings, this apparatus is designated by the reference numeral 10 (FIG. 1). The apparatus 10 includes a ground engaging base member 20, an elongated arm 30 pivotally secured to the base member 20 and a bearing platform 40 pivotally secured to the free end of the elongated arm 30.

The ground engaging base member 20 is preferably U-shaped in cross section, having upstanding side portions 21. Secured to the bottom of the base member 20 are a plurality of angles 22, the purpose of the angle 22 being to provide frictional engagement with the ground. It should be understood that other means could be provided for such frictional engagement with the ground to prevent the base member 20 from sliding across the ground during use. A pair of pins 25 are rotatably mounted within the upstanding portions 21 of the U-shaped base member near one of its ends. These pins include heads 26 at one end and threaded portions at their other end. The purpose of these pins will be more fully described hereinafter.

The elongated arm member 30 includes four rigid bars 31, two such bars pivotally secured at each side of the base member 20 near one end thereof in pantographic arrangement. The pins 25 extend through the lower extremities of the bars 31 and through the upstanding side portions 21 of the base 20, the bars being rotatable about the pins (FIGS. 1 and 3). The nuts 28 secure the pins in position, thereby pivotally securing the bars 31 to the base member 20.

A biasing platform 40 is pivotally secured to the free end of the elongated arm 30 at the other extremities of the bars 31. The bearing platform 40 is preferably of inverted U-shape, thereby including the depending flanges 41. An upstanding stop member 42 is rigidly secured to the top of platform 40. Pins 43, similar to pins 25 described hereinbefore, extend through the other extremities of the bars 31 on one side of the apparatus 10, through the depending flanges 41 and through the bars 31 on the other side of the apparatus 10. The nuts 44 are then threaded on the pins 43 thereby pivotally securing the bearing platform 40 to the elongated arm member 30.

A stop member 50 is positioned between the upstanding portions 21 of the U-shaped base member 20 near the end opposite from where the elongated arm member 30 is pivotally attached. The purpose of the stop member 50 in combination with the other structure described will now be disclosed in detail upon describing the operation of the apparatus 10.

Turning specifically to FIG. 2, the bumper of an automobile is designated by the letter B. When an automobile is immovable under its own power because the rear tires are positioned in a rut, the apparatus 10 is placed in the position shown in full lines in FIG. 2, the platform 40 being placed under the bumper and the upstanding stop member 42 bearing against the back of the bumper. The lower portion of the bumper jack 1 is positioned between the upstanding portion 21 of the base member 20 and against the upstanding stop member 50. The protruding finger 6 of the bumper jack 1 is positioned under the bearing platform 40 between the depending flanges 41. It will now be noted that upon operation of the bumper jack 1 the bearing platform 40 will be lifted upwardly and forwardly to the position shown in dotted lines in FIG. 2 with the elongated arm 30 being substantially perpendicular to the base member 20. This also of course raises the bumper B upwardly and forwardly. Upon further operation of the bumper jack, the platform 40 will pass to the position shown in dotted lines at the extreme left of FIG. 2, moving the bumper B downwardly and still further forwardly. Actually, when the elongated arm 30 passes the point where it is perpendicular to the base member 20, the weight of the automobile will move the arm 30 to the extreme forward position shown in FIG. 2.

Thus, with this simple operation, the automobile has been lifted out of the rut and moved a substantial distance forward. In practically every instance, the automobile can then be moved under its own power since it is no longer in the rut which prevented its movement in the first place. By these simple steps, the necessity of being towed out of a rut has in most cases been eliminated.

This invention provides a means whereby an automobile may be moved out of a rut, the apparatus especially well adapted to be used in combination with a bumper jack which is standard equipment in most automobiles. The apparatus performs this function quickly and simply enough so that anyone who can operate a bumper jack can operate this apparatus. It is small and compact and therefore can be carried at all times in the trunk of an automobile. It is simple in construction and therefore practically trouble free.

While only one embodiment of this invention has been shown and described, it is possible that the invention may be practiced through the use of certain other embodiments without departing from the spirit and scope of the invention. These other embodiments are to be included within the scope of this invention unless the following claims specifically state otherwise.

I claim:

1. Apparatus for moving a vehicle for use in combination with a bumper jack, said apparatus comprising: a ground engaging member; an elongated member pivotally connected to said ground engaging member; means on said elongated member for bearing against and supporting the vehicle; and means on said ground engaging member and said elongated member for receiving the bumper jack therebetween whereby said elongated member may be pivoted about said pivotal connection, past a vertical position, by the bumper jack.
2. Apparatus for moving a vehicle for use in combination with a bumper jack, said apparatus comprising: a ground engaging member; an elongated member pivotally connected at one of its ends to said ground engaging member; a bearing surface pivotally connected to the other end of said elongated member for bearing against and supporting the vehicle; and means on said ground engaging member and said elongated member for receiving the bumper jack therebetween whereby said elongated member may be pivoted about said pivotal connection to said ground engaging member, past a vertical position, by the bumper jack.
3. Apparatus for moving a vehicle for use in combination with a bumper jack, said apparatus comprising: a ground engaging base member; an elongated arm member pivotally connected at one of its extremities to said ground engaging base member near one of its ends; a bearing platform pivotally connected to the other extremity of said arm member, said bearing platform shaped to bear against and support the vehicle; and means near the other end of said ground engaging member for receiving the lower portion of a bumper jack whereby the bumper jack is received between said means and said bearing platform for pivoting said elongated member about its pivotal connection to said base member, past a vertical position, by the bumper jack.
4. Apparatus for moving a vehicle as defined in claim 3, said elongated arm member including a pair of bars in pantographic arrangement.

5. Apparatus for moving a vehicle for use in combination with a bumper jack, said apparatus comprising: a U-shaped ground engaging base member; an elongated arm member pivotally connected at one of its extremities to the upstanding portions of said U-shaped base member near one of its ends; a bearing platform pivotally connected to the other extremity of said arm member, said bearing platform shaped to bear against and support the vehicle; and an upstanding stop member positioned between said upstanding portions near the other end of said U-shaped ground engaging base member for receiving the lower portion of a bumper jack whereby the bumper jack is received between said upstanding stop member and said bearing platform for pivoting said elongated member about its pivotal connection to said base member, past a vertical position, by the bumper jack.
6. Apparatus for moving a vehicle as defined in claim 5, said elongated arm member including a pair of bars in pantographic arrangement.
7. Apparatus for moving a vehicle for use in combination with a bumper jack, said apparatus comprising: a U-shaped ground engaging base member; means on the bottom of said base member for frictional engagement with the ground; an elongated arm member including a pair of bars in pantographic arrangement each pivotally connected at one of its extremities to the upstanding portions of said U-shaped ground engaging base member near one of its ends; a bearing platform pivotally connected to the other extremity of said arm member for bearing against and supporting the vehicle; an upstanding stop means on the top of said bearing platform; and an upstanding stop member positioned between said upstanding portions near the other end of said U-shaped ground engaging base member for receiving the lower portion of a bumper jack whereby the bumper jack is received between said upstanding stop member and said bearing platform for pivoting said elongated arm member about its pivotal connection to said base member, past a vertical position, by the bumper jack.
8. Apparatus for moving a vehicle for use in combination with a bumper jack, said apparatus comprising: a U-shaped ground engaging base member; means on the bottom of said base member for frictional engagement with the ground; an elongated arm member including a pair of bars in pantographic arrangement on each side of said base member, each bar pivotally connected at one of its extremities to a pin rotatably mounted in the upstanding portions of said U-shaped ground engaging base member near one of its ends; an inverted U-shaped bearing platform, the other extremities of each of said bars of said elongated arm member pivotally secured to a pin rotatably mounted in the depending flanges of said inverted U-shaped bearing platform; an upstanding stop means on the top

of said bearing platform; and an upstanding stop member positioned between said upstanding portions near the other end of said U-shaped ground engaging base member for receiving the lower portion of a bumper jack whereby the bumper jack is received between said upstanding stop member and said bearing platform for pivoting said elongated arm member about its pivotal connection to said base member, past a vertical position, by the bumper jack.

References Cited in the file of this patent

UNITED STATES PATENTS

827,406	Austin	July 31, 1906
1,508,154	Bellamy	Sept. 9, 1924
2,361,690	Hunz	Oct. 31, 1944
2,433,537	Ward	Dec. 30, 1947
2,743,903	Lucker	May 1, 1956

116,157

July 30, 1963 — C. C. NIXON — **3,099,435**

BUMPER JACK PUSHER EXTENSION

Filed June 9, 1961

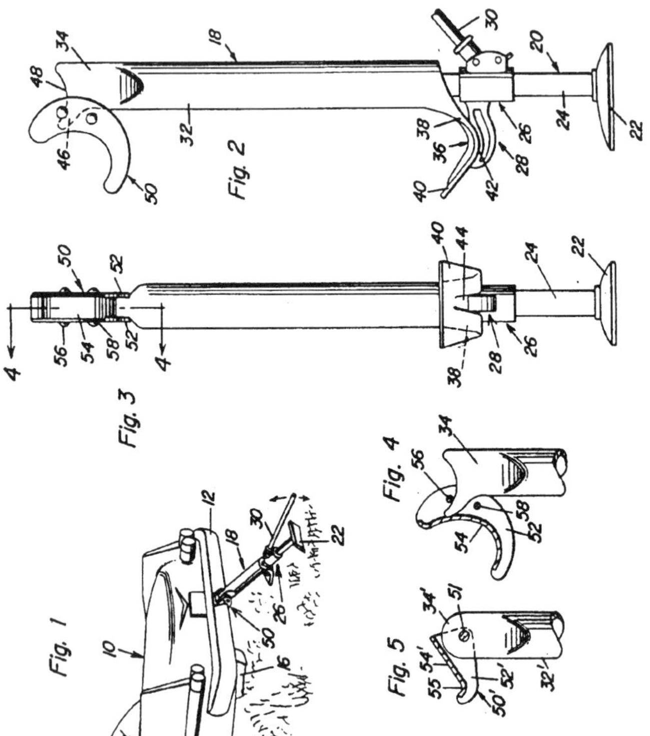

Carl C. Nixon
INVENTOR.

BY Clarence A. O'Brien and Harvey B. Jacobson
Attorneys

UNITED STATES PATENT OFFICE

3,099,435

Patented July 30,1963

CARL C. NIXON, PONTIAC, MICH.
(3522 W. Home Ave., Flint 4, Mich.

BUMPER JACK PUSHER EXTENSION

Filed June 9, 1961, Ser. No. 116,157
10 Claims. (Cl. 254—35)

This invention relates to a novel and useful bumper jack pusher extension and is in the form of an upstanding elongated tubular member adapted to be telescoped over the upper end of a bumper jack standard remote from the base thereof. The lower end of the tubular member is provided with means adapted to be seated in the upwardly opening bumper jack hook carried by the lift frame which is mounted on the standard of the bumper jack for movement there along and a reaction thrust member defining an upwardly opening and transversely extending concave recess is carried by the upper end of the elongated tubular member and is adapted to embracingly engage a vehicle bumper engage a vehicle bumper. Bumper jacks are conventionally provided with enlarged bases at the lower ends of their standards and if a vehicle has become stuck in a ditch the bumper jack extension of the instant invention is telescoped over the upper end of the conventional bumper jack standard. Then, the reaction thrust member carried by the upper end of the tubular member is engaged with the bumper of the vehicle while the base of the bumper jack is engaged with the ground. Thus as the lift frame of the bumper jack is jacked along the standard of the bumper jack, it will extend the tubular member telescoped over the upper end of the bumper jack standard thereby changing the conventional bumper jack into an extensible motor having a reaction thrust surface on one end defined by the reaction thrust member carried by the bumper jack extension and a reaction thrust member carried by the bumper jack extension and a reaction thrust surface on the other end defined by the base of the jack standard. Although the bumper jack extension of the instant invention has been specifically adapted for use with vehicles, it may be readily appreciated that the extension, when used in conjunction with a bumper jack, may readily find use in other environments.

The main object of this invention is to provide a bumper jack extension or attachment for a conventional type of bumper jack including a base, a jack standard rising from the base and a lift frame mounted on the standard for movement there along which may be used to convert a conventional bumper jack into an extensible motor with reaction thrust surfaces on the remote ends thereof.

A further object of this invention, in accordance with the immediately preceding object, is to provide a bumper jack extension provided with a reaction thrust member specifically adapted to embracingly engage a portion of a vehicle bumper.

Yet another object of this invention is to provide a tubular member of the instant invention comprising the portion of the extension which is to be telescoped over the upper end of a jack standard with a laterally directed and upwardly opening generally V-shaped plate member on its lower end adapted to be seatingly engaged in the conventional upwardly opening bumper hook carried by the lift frame on conventional bumper jacks. In this manner, the tubular member of the instant invention may be constructed of sufficient diameter to readily telescope over bumper jack standards of various sizes and shapes with the laterally directed upwardly opening V-shaped plate member seatingly engaged in the upwardly opening bumper hook provided by the lift frame of the bumper jack in order that the tubular member may be engaged by the bumper jack lift frame in a manner whereby rotational movement of the tubular member relative to the bumper jack standard is prevented.

Still another object of this invention is to provide the outer end of the upwardly opening and laterally directed V-shaped plate member with a transversely extending cutting edge whereby this cutting edge may be utilized as a cutting implement such as a grub axe when it becomes necessary to cut undergrowth in which a vehicle has become stuck.

A final object of this invention to be specifically enumerated herein is to provide a bumper jack extension which will conform to conventional forms of manufacture, be of simple construction, and easy to use so as to provide a device that will be economically feasible, long lasting, and relatively trouble free in operation.

These together with other objects and advantages which will become subsequently apparent reside in the details of construction and operation as more fully hereinafter described and claimed, reference being had to the accompanying drawings forming a part hereof, wherein like numerals refer to like parts throughout, and in which:

FIGURE 1 is a perspective view of the rear portion of a vehicle shown with the bumper jack extension and an associated bumper jack being operatively disposed relative to each other and in position to be utilized in order to effect an upward and forward thrust on the rear end of the vehicle;

FIGURE 2 is a side elevational view of a conventional type of bumper jack shown with the bumper jack extension operatively connected thereto;

FIGURE 3 is an end elevational view of the embodiment illustrated in FIGURE 2 as seen from the left side of the latter;

FIGURE 4 is a fragmentary vertical sectional view taken substantially upon the plane indicated by the section line 4—4 of FIGURE 3; and

FIGURE 5 is a vertical sectional view similar to that of FIGURE 4 but showing a modified form of bumper jack extension.

Referring now more specifically to the drawings the numeral 10 generally designates a vehicle which is provided with a rear bumper 12. The vehicle is disposed on a soft ground surface 14 and has its rear wheels 16 embedded in the ground in a manner to prevent the rear wheels 16 from effecting forward movement of the vehicle 10.

The bumper jack extension of the instant invention is generally designated by the reference numeral 18 and is illustrated in FIGURES 1-3 of the drawings operatively associated with a conventional form of bumper jack which is generally designated by the reference numeral 20. The bumper jack 20 includes an enlarged base portion 22, an upright jack standard 24 and a lift frame generally referred to by the reference numeral 26 of conventional design provided with a laterally directed and upwardly opening bumper hook generally referred to by the reference numeral 28. The lift frame 26 includes a pivotally mounted lever arm 30 which may be manipulated in order to move the lift frame 26 upwardly along the standard 20.

The bumper jack extension 18 comprises an upstanding elongated tubular member 32 which is closed at its upper end as at 34. The tubular member 18 includes an upwardly opening and laterally directed V-shaped plate member generally referred to by the reference numeral 36 which includes a first leg 38 which projects downwardly and outwardly away from the tubular member 32 and a second leg 40 that projects upwardly and outwardly away from the free end of the leg 38. With attention invited to FIGURES 2 and 3 of the drawings it will be noted that the undersurfaces of the legs 38 and 40 adjacent to the apex 42 of the V-shaped plate member 36 are provided with communicated downwardly opening grooves 44 which seatingly receive the upper surfaces of the bumper hook 28 and thus prevent rotation of the tubular member 32 relative to the standard 24.

The upper end of the tubular member 32 is provided with a laterally projecting and upwardly opening hook member 46 which defines an upwardly opening concave recess 48 that extends transversely of the tubular member 32.

A reaction thrust member generally referred to by the reference number 50 comprises a generally inverted U-shaped member having a pair of generally parallel legs 52 interconnected by means of a transversely curved bight portion 54. A pair of support pins 56 and 58 are secured between the legs 52 a spaced distance from the bight portion 54 and spaced relative to each other transversely of the bight portion 54. The hook member 46 is received between support pins 56 and 58 to rockably mount the reaction thrust member 50 on the upper end of the tubular member 32 for movement about an axis extending transversely of the hook member 46.

With attention now invited to FIGURE 5 of the drawings there will be seen a modified form of tubular member referred to by the reference numeral 32'. The upper end of the tubular member 32' is flattened as at 34' and has a reaction thrust member generally referred to by the reference numeral 50', pivotally secured thereto by means of the pivot pin 51. The reaction thrust member 50' also includes a pair of legs 52' which are interconnected by means of a transversely curved bight portion 54' and the curved end 55 of the bight portion 54' may be engaged with the bumper 12 in the same manner in which the reaction thrust member 50 is engaged with the bumper 12 in FIGURE 1. Further, the reaction thrust member 50 may be readily disengaged from the tubular member 32 and the upwardly opening concave transversely extending recess 48 may be utilized to embrace a portion of the bumper 12.

In operation, if it is desired to free a vehicle such as vehicle 10 from a position with its rear wheels 16 embedded in the ground 14, the base 22 of the jack 20 is engaged with the ground as illustrated in FIGURE 1 and the tubular member 32 is telescopingly engaged over the upper end of the jack standard 24. Then, the jack standard is forwardly and upwardly inclined and the reaction thrust member 50 is engaged with the bumper 12. Then, the lever 30 may be utilized to effect movement of the lift frame 26 upwardly along the jack standard 24 whereby the extensible motor defined by the jack 20 and the bumper jack extension 18 will effect an upward and forward thrust on the rear bumper 12 of the vehicle 10 in order to force the vehicle 10 forwardly over the soft ground 14.

The foregoing is considered as illustrative only of the principles of the invention. Further, since numerous modifications and changes will readily occur to those skilled in the art, it is not desired to limit the invention to the exact construction and operation shown and described, and accordingly all suitable modifications and equivalents may be resorted to, falling within the scope of the invention as claimed.

What is claimed as new is as follows:

1. A bumper jack extension for converting a conventional bumper jack of the type including a base, a jack standard rising from said base and an upwardly opening bumper hook on a lift frame mounted on said standard for movement there along, to an extensible motor having two telescoped sections, said bumper jack extension comprising an upstanding elongated tubular member of a size so as to be telescoped over the upper end of the bumper jack standard remote from the base thereof, the low end of said tubular member including means for seating in the upwardly opening bumper hook carried by said lift frame, and a reaction thrust member carried by the upper end of said tubular member including means for seating in the upwardly opening bumper hook carried by

said lift frame, and a reaction thrust member carried by the upper end of said tubular member for engagement with a vehicle bumper whereby said bumper jack standard may be oriented upwardly and in the direction of desired movement of a disabled vehicle with said base engaged with the ground and said reaction thrust member engaged with the bumper of said disabled vehicle said upper end of said tubular member including at least one laterally projecting hook member defining an upwardly opening concave recess.

2. The combination of claim 1 wherein said reaction thrust member comprises a generally inverted U-shaped member having a pair of generally parallel legs interconnected at corresponding ends by means of a transversely curved bight portion, a pair of support pins secured between said legs spaced from said bight portion and spaced relative to each other transversely of said bight portion between which said hook member is loosely and removably received for mounting said reaction thrust member on said tubular member.
3. A bumper jack extension for converting a conventional bumper jack of the type including a base, a jack standard rising from said base and an upwardly opening bumper hook on a lift frame mounted on said standard for movement therealong, to an extensible motor having two telescoped sections, said bumper jack extension comprising an upstanding elongated tubular member of a size so as to be telescoped over the upper end of the bumper jack standard remote from the base thereof, the lower end of said tubular member including means for seating in the upwardly opening bumper hook carried by said lift frame, and a reaction thrust member carried by the upper end of said tubular member for engagement with a vehicle bumper whereby said bumper jack standard may be orientated upwardly and in the direction of desired movement of a disabled vehicle with said base engaged with the ground and said reaction thrust member engaged with the bumper of said disabled vehicle, said reaction thrust member defining an arcuate pocket extending transversely of said tubular member and opening toward the upper end thereof.
4. The combination of claim 3 wherein said reaction thrust member is rockably mounted on said upper end of said tubular member for movement about an axis extending transversely thereof.
5. The combination of claim 4 including means limiting rocking movement of said reaction thrust member.
6. The combination of claim 3 wherein said means adapted for seating engagement with said bumper hook comprises an upwardly opening laterally directed V-shaped plate member having one leg thereof extending outwardly and downwardly from said tubular member with the other

leg thereof extending upwardly and outwardly from the free end of said one leg.

7. The combination of claim 6 wherein the undersurfaces of said legs each have a downwardly opening groove formed therein adjacent the apex of said V-shaped plate member adapted for seatingly receiving the upper surfaces of said bumper hook.
8. The combination of claim 3 wherein said reaction thrust member is pivotally secured to the tubular member.
9. A bumper jack extension for converting a conventional bumper jack of the type including a base, a jack standard rising from said base, and an upwardly opening bumper hook on a lift frame mounted on said standard for movement there along, to an extensible motor having two telescoped sections, said bumper jack extension comprising an upstanding elongated tubular member of a size so as to be telescoped over the upper end of the bumper jack standard remote from the base thereof, the lower end of said tubular member including means for seating in the upwardly opening bumper hook carried by said lift frame, said means comprising an upwardly opening laterally directed V-shaped plate member having one leg thereof extending outwardly and downwardly from said tubular member with the other leg thereof extending upwardly and outwardly from the free end of said one leg, the upper end of said tubular member being adapted for carrying a reaction thrust member engageable with a vehicle bumper, said reaction thrust member to define an arcuate pocket extending transversely of said tubular member and opening toward the upper end thereof, whereby said bumper jack standard may be orientated upwardly and in the direction of desired movement of the disabled vehicle with said base engaged with the ground and said reaction thrust member engaged with the bumper of said disabled vehicle.
10. A bumper jack extension for converting a conventional bumper jack of a type including a base, a jack standard rising from said base, and an upwardly opening bumper hook on a lift frame mounted on said standard for movement therealong, to an extension motor having two telescoped sections, said bumper jack extension comprising an upstanding elongated tubular member of a size so as to be telescoped over the upper end of the bumper jack standard remote from the base thereof, the lower end of said tubular member including means for seating in the upwardly opening bumper hook carried by said lift frame, said means comprising an upwardly opening laterally directed V-shaped plate member having one leg thereof extending outwardly and downwardly from said tubular member with the other leg thereof extending upwardly and outwardly from the free end of said one leg, the undersurfaces of said legs each

having a downwardly opening groove formed therein adjacent the apex of said V-shaped plate member for seatingly receiving the upper surfaces of said bumper hook, and the upper end of said tubular member being adapted to carry a reaction thrust member for engagement with a vehicle bumper whereby said bumper jack standard may be orientated upwardly and in the direction of the desired movement of a disabled vehicle with said base engaged with the ground and said reaction thrust member engaged with the bumper of said disabled vehicle.

References Cited in the file of this patent
UNITED STATES PATENTS

1,482,846	Harrah	Feb. 5, 1924
1,648,188	Maltrup	Nov. 8, 1927
1,805,289	Kuno	May 12, 1931
1,845,222	Birn	Feb. 16, 1932
2,259,789	Akins	Oct. 21, 1941

United States Patent [19]

Stickle, Jr.

[11] **4,025,053**

[45] **May 24, 1977**

[54] **SCREW ACTUATED SCISSOR JACK WITH A SELF ADJUSTING BEARING SURFACE**

[76] Inventor: **Warren Edward Stickle, Jr.**, 134 Somerset St., Somerville, N.J. 08876

[22] Filed: **May 10, 1976**

[21] Appl. No.: **684,541**

[52] **U.S. Cl.** .... **254/122**; 254/126; 254/133 R; 254/DIG. 4

[51] **Int. Cl.**[2] **B66F 3/22**

[58] **Field of Search** .... 254/122, 126, 9 R, 9 B, 254/9 C, 133, 134, DIG. 4

[56] **References Cited**

UNITED STATES PATENTS

2,546,361	3/1951	Floyd	254/126
2,929,519	3/1960	Taylor	254/9 C
2,931,519	4/1960	Beach	254/134

FOREIGN PATENTS OR APPLICATIONS

1,195,412	5/1959	France

Primary Examiner—Al Lawrence Smith
Assistant Examiner—Robert C. Watson
Attorney, Agent, or Firm—Henry J. Walsh

[57] **ABSTRACT**

There is disclosed a scissor-type screw actuated jack arrangement having a floating load bearing plate centrally situated over supporting lift arms when in the fully extended position and a pair of facing U-shaped channel members coupled to opposite ends of the lift arms for carrying the bearing plate and screw.

3 Claims, 5 Drawing Figures

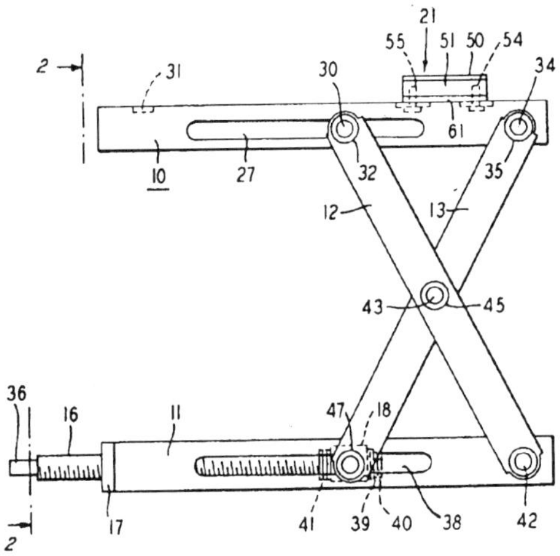

FIG. 1

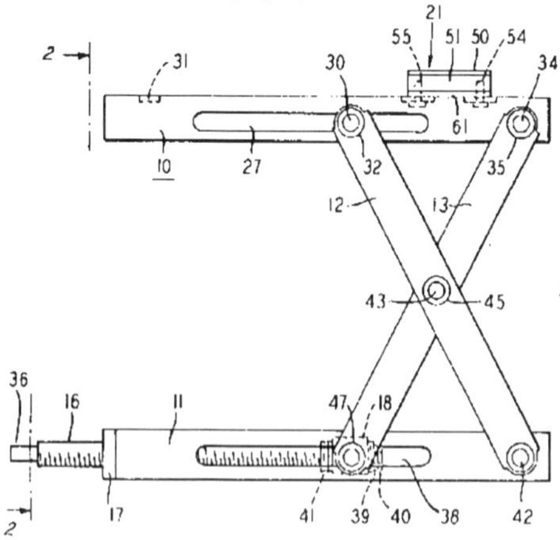

FIG. 2

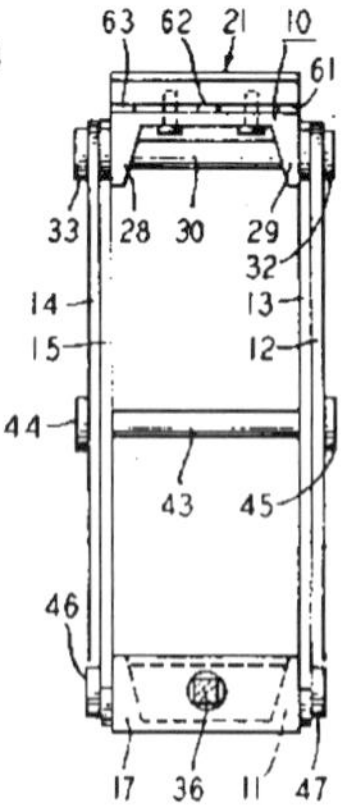

FIG. 3

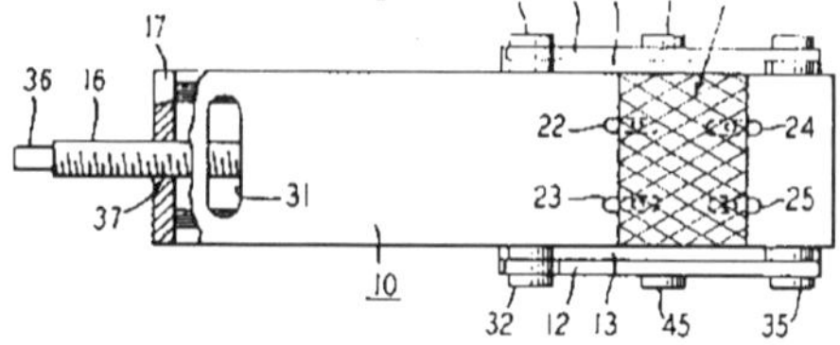

FIG. 5

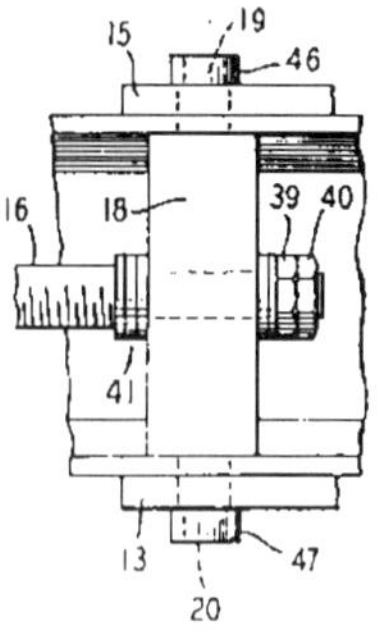

FIG. 4

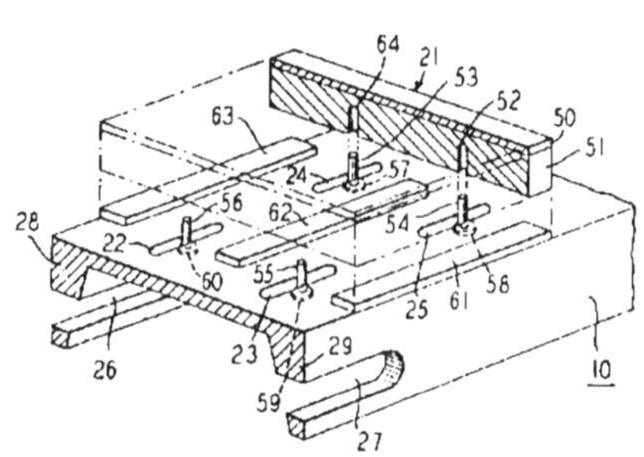

SCREW ACTUATED SCISSOR JACK WITH A SELF ADJUSTING BEARING SURFACE

Background of the Invention

This invention pertains to portable devices for raising and sustaining for long periods in a raised position parts of machines, and more particularly, to an improved and strengthened scissor jack for lifting automobiles or tractors from a position beneath such parts.

As is well known, automotive parts such as engines, transmissions, differentials, etc., are generally too heavy to be lifted without some mechanical assistance. In addition, it is frequently impossible to lift these parts from above by a hoist or overhead lifting device because such parts are inaccessible, or because a breakdown has occurred in some remote place. Therefore, it has become fairly common to use a lifting jack which, when fully collapsed, can be placed easily under a car and raised from that position to lift the car or any part thereof off the ground.

Generally, portable jacks which may be transported in the trunk of an automobile and are widely available to the consuming public, are characteristically made for emergency use rather than everyday use. These jacks employ compromising design structures which will fatigue if used repeatedly. Some of these portable jacks represent substantial hazards to the user because of improper designs which can cause the jack to shift off center in actual use.

Accordingly, it is an object of this invention to provide an improved jack design that is both strong, stable, an durable which can be produced in quantities at relatively low costs.

It is also an object of this invention to furnish a portable scissor jack which compensates for shifts in a lifted load thereby avoiding tilting, or off-center, loads from prematurely collapsing the jack.

Summary of the Invention

These as well as other objects are accomplished in the preferred embodiment of my invention, disclosed in detail hereinafter, which includes two channel members held in spaced relationship by pairs of scissor lifting arms which are screw actuated. The top channel member carries a floating load bearing platform which rides on lubricated metal strips and is movable a limited distance constrained by integral downwardly extending stop pins stationed in elongated openings of the top member. The floating platform is designed to carry the load and is approximately centrally situated over the lifting arms when in the fully extended position. The bottom channel serves as the base support for the jack providing a relatively large surface in contact with the surface to improve stability.

Brief Description of the Drawing

Referring now to the drawing, the objects and features of the invention can be better appreciated from a careful consideration of the drawing which includes:

FIG. 1 depicting a side view of my jack arrangement in almost a fully extended position;

FIG. 2 showing a front view taken along section lines 2—2 of FIG. 1 to depict the hand crank adapter at the bottom thereof as well as the axles supporting the lifting arms;

FIG. 3 showing a top view of the jack displaying to the right side of the figure the load bearing platform in relation to the lifting screw;

FIG. 4 depicting in section line outline the shape of the platform as well as the supporting arrangement thereof; and

FIG. 5 showing the screw joined to a transverse axle for translating horizontal displacement to vertical lift displacement.

Detailed Description

Considering FIG. 1 initially, it discloses a top U-shaped channel member 10 supported above a similarly shaped, but inverted, channel member 11 which serves as a base. U-shaped channel members were chosen in my design because of their known resistance to bending with off-set load and to other distortions, such as twisting. A profile end view of member 10 may be best seen in FIG. 2. Member 10 is supported apart from (or close to) member 11 by pairs of lifting arms 12 and 13, and arms 14 and 15. In FIG. 1, arms 12 and 13 are easily seen, but arms 14 and 15, which are aligned directly behind them, cannot be seen. The symmetrical positioning of these pairs of lifting mechanisms can be appreciated from the view in FIG. 2.

Member 11 carries threaded shaft 16 which is in threaded engagement with threaded plate 17 and bottom forward axle 18. The latter is largely blocked from view in FIG. 1 by the bottom portion of arm 13, but may be seen in FIG. 5 in a cutaway section showing shaft 16, axle 18 and arms 13 and 15 together with force-fitting caps 19 and 20. The latter can be replaced by any suitable fastener, e.g., nut and washer arrangement. The horizontal section of U-shaped member 11 touches the ground when in use and serves as the base support for the jack. Its relatively large surface improves the stability of the jack.

Sitting atop member 10 is bearing platform 21 which has diamond shaped etching (see FIG. 3) on its top surface to improve surface friction. Platform 21 is movably mounted on member 10, as will be described in greater detail hereinafter. Platform 21 engages the load to be lifted, and advantageously, in accordance with a feature of this invention, it is movable guided along elongated openings in member 10. As will be discussed in further detail, these openings, numbered 22-25, are shown in FIG. 4.

It should be noted that five axles (number 18, 30, 34, 42, and 43) are used at each pivot or slide to give maximum lateral stability to the design and to afford built-in low friction bearings which tend to rotate as the jack is raised or lowered.

The advantage of the mobility of platform 21 may be appreciated if we consider the problems of lifting a car bumper to change a tire. The jack is placed under the car frame nearest the tire to be removed. As the jack lifts the car, one corner of the car tilts upward, but the other tires remain in contact with the ground. In actual fact, the load contact (touching platform 21) being a fixed distance from the tires in contact with the ground, travels through an arc, and does not move truly vertically up and down. While it is true that the radius of the arc is large relatively speaking, there is a slight horizontal displacement. As the car is lifted higher, the displacement increases and eventually the jack tilts and falls. The car brakes are ordinarily left unset to allow for this problem, but that solution is manifestly hazardous. In this arrangement, platform 21 moves to compensate for the displacement of the load.

Returning to the detailed consideration, member 10 has a pair of top guide slots 26 and 27 midway along downwardly projecting legs 28 and 29. Slot 27 is visible in FIG. 1 and portions of both slots 26 and 27 may be seen in FIG. 4. Slots 26 and 27 are of equal length and size, and are symmetrically positioned along respective legs 28 and 29. Slots 26 and 27 serve as guides and stops for top forward axle 30 (see FIG. 2). As shown in FIG. 1, the jack is approximately 80 percent of its full height which is reached when forward axle 30 is positioned at the extreme right side of slots 26 and 27. Axle 30 is rotatably mounted to arms 12 and 15 by fastener collars 32 and 33.

Member 10 has a cutout 31 (seen best in FIG. 1) which is used as a convenient grip to move the jack when collapsed. Advantageously, when the jack is fully collapsed (axle 30 moved to extreme left position of slot 27), member 10 is nearly in touching relationship to member 11, providing a convenient assembly for storage until needed.

Member 10 is also fitted with a rearward axle 34 rotatably mounted in openings (not shown) therein. Axle 34 is held in position by collars (collar 35 only can be seen) which also hold lift arms 13 and 15 at their respective upper ends allowing them to pivotally rotate axle 34.

Lift arms 12 and 13 cooperate with lift arms 14 and 15 to translate the horizontal displacement of threaded shaft, or screw, 16 into transverse displacement of member 10 with respect to member 11. Threaded shaft 16 has a reduced diameter at one end which has been given the shape of a rectangular adapter 36 suitable to fit conventional hand cranks. As shaft 16 is turned it advances horizontally (to right for raising and to left for lowering) and axle 18 which is secured as shown in FIG. 5, also moves horizontally along bottom guide slot 38 and a mating guide slot opposite it in member 11. Axle 18 is secured to shaft 16 as shown by a pair of nuts 39 and 40 (acting together as a lock nut) and oil-less bearing thrust washer 41. Thus, as axle 28 moves restrained by rear axle 42 and central axle 43 and their respective assemblies, the scissor formed by arms 12 and 13 opens (lowers) and closes (lifts).

Turning our attention now to FIG. 4 and to platform 21, we can see in phantom outline the shape of top plate 50 secured to block 51, Platform 21 rides on three bronze strips 61-63 which have been impregnated by a lubricant which is released in small but sufficient amounts under load. Plate 50 may be composed of hardened metals which are uniquely adapted to the expected load stresses. There are four bottom drill holes in block 51 (only holes 52 and 64 are shown) positioned to receive stop pins 53-56. During assembly, pins 53-56 are fitted in block 51 and block 51 is positioned so that pins 53-56 protrude downwardly into openings 22-25. Stop collars 57-60 are inserted (force-fitted), welded, or otherwise permanently secured to pins 53-56 to prevent removal of platform 21 from member 10. Obviously, pins 53-56 and collars 57-60 could be made as unitary assemblies, if desired, and driven (or screwed, if block 51 is priorly taped) into block 51. These, as well as other variations are believed to be within the scope and spirit of the disclosed invention.

I claim:

1. A scissor jack arrangement comprising a pair of facing plate members relatively movable toward and away from each other, pairs of arms pivotally joined at their respective midsections and at their rearward lower and upper ends to ends of said plate members, forward ends of said pairs of arms being slidably joined to each of said facing plate members through an elongated slot opening associated therewith, an axle running transverse to said pairs of arms and slidable connected to each forward lower end of each of said arms, a threaded plate at an end opposite to where said rearward arm is pivotally joined to a lower one of said plate members, a threaded shaft being threaded into said threaded plate and fixedly secured to said axle for movement of forward and rearward ends of said respective arms toward and away from each other, a floating loadbearing platform slidably mounted on a top one of said plate members for movement longitudinally therealong, and said platform includes downwardly extend-

ing securement pins interfitted with elongated apertures in said top plate member situated substantially centrally between said pair of arms, and lubricating strips running longitudinally between said top plate member and said platform for self-lubricating movement of said platform.

2. A scissor jack assembly comprising an upper load-bearing plate member and a lower plate member joined by a pair of collapsible scissor structures;

each of said scissor structures including a pair of arms pivotally joined at their respective midsections, end sections of said arms on each of said structures being pivotally joined to rearward sections on said bearing plate member and said lower plate member, and opposite end sections of said arms on each of said structures being slidably joined to opposite plate members;

a threaded shaft being fixedly secured to the opposite end sections of said arms on each of said structures;

a mating threaded member secured to said lower plate member for relative movement of said bearing plate member with respect to said lower plate member as said threaded shaft is turned engaged in said mating threaded member;

a floating load bearing platform slidably mounted on said load-bearing plate member for restricted movement therealong; and lubricating strips between said upper load-bearing plate member and said platform for self-lubricating movement of said platform.

3. The invention recited in claim 2 further including securement pins projecting downwardly from said load-bearing plate member, and interfitting elongated apertures in said upper load-bearing plate member for restricted motion of said platform.

United States Patent [19]

LeVert

[11] **4,218,043**

[45] **Aug. 19, 1980**

[54] **MANUAL AUTOMOBILE PUSHER**

[76] Inventor: **Francis E. LeVert**, 1909 Matthew La., Knoxville, Tenn. 37919

[21] Appl. No.: **11,174**

[22] Filed: **Feb. 9, 1979**

[51] **Int. Cl.**³ **B66F 1/04**

[52] **U.S. Cl.** **254/35**; 254/108; 254/134; 254/DIG. 1; 254/DIG. 4

[58] **Field of Search** .... 254/1, 35, 95–97, 254/108–111, 120, 124, 126, 129–130, 131, 133, 134, DIG. 1, DIG. 4

[56] **References Cited**

U.S. PATENT DOCUMENTS

486,528	11/1892	Bryant et al.	254/133
1,325,964	12/1919	Templeton	254/111
1,821,627	9/1931	Fotheringham	254/126
2,144,303	1/1939	Wiedman	254/DIG. 1
3,029,065	4/1962	Buddingh	254/35
3,099,435	7/1963	Nixon	254/35
4,025,053	5/1977	Stickle	254/133 R

Primary Examiner—Robert C. Watson

[57] **ABSTRACT**

A manual automobile pusher comprises a long handle ratchet mechanism mounted on one end of a curved hollow rectangular shaped sleeve, a padded cradle connected to the opposite end of the rectangular shaped sleeve, a curved rack post along which the ratchet mechanism and hollow rectangular shaped sleeve moves, a broad base which is connected to the curved rack post by a pivot pin, and an extensible cross member that is firmly connected to the broad base and the hollow rectangular shaped sleeve. The manual car pusher is capable of developing sufficient horizontal and vertical forces to slowly push an automobile out of a rut in ice, snow or mud, thereby eliminating the waste of gasoline and automobile transmission wear that occurs when a lone driver attempts to free an immobile vehicle by driving it out of a rut.

1 Claim, 1 Drawing Figure

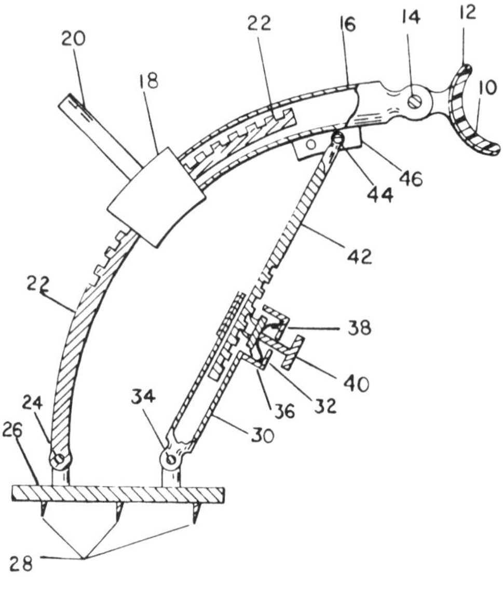

MANUAL AUTOMOBILE PUSHER

Background of the Invention

This invention relates to the extrication of immobile automobiles when one or more tires are trapped in ruts in ice, snow, or mud such that driving wheels traction is not enough to develop motion of the vehicle.

There are several well-known means for removing an automobile from ruts in mud, snow, or ice These involve the use of rock, salt, abrasive such as sand or gravel, rocking motion brought about by rapid changes in the gears of the automobile from forward to reverse, manual pushing, and tow trucks equipped with mechanical winches. Of these methods, the most successful involves the use of tow trucks equipped with mechanical winches. But during periods of severe weather conditions it is difficult to secure the service of a tow truck with winching capabilities. Thus, most often, motorists resort to one of the first four methods. The rocking motion method is the most frequently used technique. Unfortunately, it is also the one method which results in the waste of gasoline and wear and tear on the tires and transmission of the vehicle. Manual pushing, which requires more than one person, is frequently successful but it involves the risk of bodily injury and also a considerable waste of gasoline as the driver attempts to aid the human pushers.

It would be useful to have a device that an average individual could use to extricate an immobile vehicle from an ice, snow, or mud rut and that would be small and lightweight enough to be inserted in the trunk of an automobile. It is an object of the present invention to provide a method and means of extricating a vehicle from a rut. It is a further object of the present invention to make a lightweight and portable automobile pusher.

Other objects of this invention will become obvious in the course of the detailed description.

Detailed Description of the Invention

FIG. 1 is a sectional view of the invention.

In FIG. 1, rubber cradle 10 is mounted as by adhesive to curved high strength aluminum cradle 12. The rubber cradle and the high strength aluminum cradle 10 and 12, respectively, are designed to make a firm high friction contact with either the front or rear bumper of an average automobile. Said aluminum cradle 12 is connected as by steel pivot 14 to curved hollow rectangular metal sleeve 16. The contact surfaces between said aluminum cradle 12 and the hollow rectangular metal sleeve 16 are designed with matching teeth so as to make the angle between the two adjustable. Said hollow rectangular metal sleeve 16 is designed with a 145.54 centimeter radius of curvature, a 2.54 centimeter width, a 3.84 centimeter height and a wall thickness of 0.80 centimeters. The arc length of said hollow rectangular metal sleeve 16 is 46 centimeters. Ratchet mechanism 18 is rigidly connected to said hollow rectangular metal sleeve 16 such that the ratchet and said hollow rectangular metal sleeve 16 form a continuous rectangular sleeve. Said ratchet mechanism 18 consists of an ordinary automobile jack mechanism. Said ratchet mechanism 18 is operated by metal bar 20 and moves along rack post 22. The rack post 22 is constructed of iron and is rectangular in shape with a radius of curvature equal to that of said hollow rectangular metal sleeve 16. Said rack post 22 is connected as by smooth steel pin 24 to metal rectangular base 26. Metal studs 28 are mounted on the observe side of the metal rectangular base 26 and are designed to prevent slippage on a surface that may be 100% ice. Hollow metal cylinder 30 on which is mounted spring loaded mechanism 32 is connected as by smooth pivot pin 34 to the metal rectangular base 26. The spring loaded mechanism 32 is composed of iron stopper 36 which is mounted against steel spring 38, and engage/disengage lever 40. When said spring loaded mechanism 32 is engaged as by the lever 40, the iron stopper 36 makes firm contact with rack post 42 allowing movement of the rack post 42 in one direction. Said rack post 42 is connected by smooth pivot pin 44 to metal anchor 46 which is rigidly connected to said hollow rectangular metal sleeve 16. The anchor 46 is designed such that the device may be adjusted for different bumper heights above a surface. Said rack post 22 and said hollow rectangular metal sleeve 16 are of rectangular cross sections; however, they could equally as well be triangular, square, or round in cross sectional shape. Said metal rectangular base 26, also, could equally as well be a triangular or curved metal plate with edges designed to prevent slippage under load. While the present invention makes use of said ratchet mechanism 18 to perform the mechanical work, the mechanical work could equally as well be performed by a worm gear - rack post combination such as commonly used in automobile jacks.

To operate the invention of FIG. 1, a person would be required to exert less than 88 newtons of force on the metal bar 20 (if its length is greater than or equal to 41 centimeters) to move a 1362 kg mass automobile with inflated tires that has become immobile with its rear wheels in an ice, snow, or mud rut. The principle of operation of this invention is based on the operation of said ratchet mechanism 36 driven by said metal bar 20 such that a small force applied on said metal bar 20 results in the application of a large force to the bumper of an automobile. The force on the automobile bumper has both horizontal and vertical components. The horizontal force provides most of the pushing force while the vertical component provides a lifting force on the automobile.

The embodiments of the invention in which an exclusive property at privilege is claimed are defined as follows:

1. A device for freeing automobiles form ice, snow, or mud ruts, the device comprising:

a rubber cradle;
a metal cradle connected to the rubber cradle;
a curved hollow rectangular metal sleeve connected with nonslippage contact to the metal cradle as by a smooth steel pivot pin;
a ratchet mechanism connected to the curved hollow rectangular metal sleeve;
a curved solid metal rack post with identical radius of curvature as said hollow rectangular metal sleeve designed to mate with the mechanism;
a metal rectangular base connected to the curved rack post by a smooth steel pivot pin;
a set of metal studs mounted on the metal rectangular base to prevent slippage;
a telescoping metal strut connected to both said metal rectangular base and to said hollow rectangular metal sleeve by a smooth steel pin;
a spring loaded mechanism mounted on said telescoping metal strut;
a hand operated lever with two positions to engage or disengage the spring loaded mechanism.

Glossary

Abandonment: 1. Means that the inventor has lost or waived his or her right to patent protection by:

A. *Actual abandonment*—Express words to the effect that he or she does not intend to seek patent protection; express disclaimer of subject matter already patented; or reissue of patent with narrower claims. (See *Disclaimer, Reissue.*)
B. *Implied abandonment*—Unreasonable delay in applying for patent without justification for delay, as in the case of a trade secret, or failure to claim part of invention in a patent issued on such invention.
C. *Constructive abandonment*—One year public use or sale before filing application; one year disclosure in patent or printed publication before filing application; prior patenting in a foreign country on application filed more than 12 months prior to filing U.S. application; or failure to present claims until more than one year after issue of a patent claiming same subject matter.

2. *Of application*: Delay in filing amendment beyond prescribed period from date of Official Action; failure to pay final fee within prescribed time period; express abandonment, in writing, sent to the Patent Office.

Aggregation: Arrangement of elements so as to produce no more than the mere sum of the elements. Each element remains unchanged in function or effect, and its action is unaffected, except incidentally, by the union of elements; direct opposite of "combination"; final result is the mere adding together of the separate contributions of the various component elements.

Amendment: Paper filed in the Patent Office by the applicant or his or her attorney, responding to all grounds of objection or rejection raised in the Official Action or within such shorter period as may be specified in such Action.

Anticipation: An act rendering unpatentable an invention owing to:

1. Prior invention, knowledge, or use of substantially the same complete and operative device or method in the United States and making it accessible to the public preceding the date of the invention; or

2. A prior patent or printed publication, or combination of patents and/or publications, containing disclosure sufficiently complete to permit one skilled in the particular art to which the invention relates to produce the invention without the exercise of inventive skill, having effective dates prior to the date of the invention.

Applicant: The person or persons in whose name the patent application is filed. The applicant becomes the patentee upon issue of the patent.

Application: The disclosure filed in the Patent Office upon which a patent is issued: consists of an abstract, summary, background discussion, a brief description of the figures, detailed specifications, claim or claims, and an oath. The claims particularly constitute the subject matter that the applicant regards as his or her invention.

Art: Three meanings are commonly attached to this term in connection with patents:

1. An operation or series of operations to secure a desired result; synonymous with the words "process," "method," and "mode of treatment."
2. A general term used to refer to patents or printed publications, e.g., "prior art," "art of record," etc.
3. A general term for a particular field of endeavor, e.g., "art of metal working."

Claims: That portion of a patent which spells out the area of protection afforded the patentee; forms an essential part of the specification as originally filed.

Combination: Opposite of "aggregation"; the individual elements are functionally related to each other in such a novel manner as to produce a new and useful result or an old result in an improved or modified manner; the combination of elements produces a different force, effect, or result from the sum produced by those elements acting alone.

Circumvention: The act of getting around an existing patent by attacking that patent in its weak claims. A dominant claim with detail is at great risk for circumvention.

Commercial use: Placing an invention in actual use for other than experimental purposes even though experiments continue; term in general applied to mean "public use," which constitutes a bar to granting of a valid patent if carried out more than one year prior to the filing of a patent application on such invention. (See *Public use.*)

Conception: The formation in the mind of the inventor of a definite and concrete idea of the complete and operative invention as it is thereafter to be applied in practice. It should be understood that conception is not the perception or realization of the means by which the result can be produced. Conception may be considered as consisting of two parts:

1. The idea that a certain desired result may be obtained by following a particular general plan; and
2. The selection of the means for effectively carrying out the idea.

The inventive concept may reside in either or both of the above two parts.

Diligence: The activity of an inventor in bringing about a reduction to practice of his or her invention; becomes important in an interference (see *Interference*), where the party who was first to conceive the invention did not reduce it to practice until after his or her opponent had already done so. (See *Priority*.)

Disclaimer: A remedy available to a patentee that permits him or her to narrow the scope of protection originally granted under the patent. (See *Abandonment* (1) (A).)

Disclosure: A full and accurate description of the invention, either by words or drawings or by model, if it be of a machine, sufficiently clear to enable one skilled in the art to reduce the invention to practical form without the exercise of the inventive faculties; complete disclosure of best embodiment known to applicant is required in a patent application. (See *Application*, *Specification*.)

Discovery: The revelation of something that exists but was heretofore unknown. (See *Invention*.)

Domination: The process of including or claiming every aspect of an invention.

Equivalent: An element, or combination of elements, that, if substituted into an existing process, device, or composition, performs substantially the same function in substantially the same way, to produce substantially the same result as that produced by the element or elements replaced.

Infringement: The unauthorized making, using, or selling of anything protected by the claims of a valid patent. (See *License*.)

Interference: A proceeding instituted by the Patent Office for the sole purpose of determining the question of priority of invention (see *Priority*) between two or more inventors; may involve two or more applicants or an applicant and a patentee.

Invention: The creation of something that did not exist before, possessing the elements of novelty, utility, etc., in a measure different from what the art might expect from the skilled worker (contrast with discovery); difficulty arises in defining the standards to be applied to measure "invention." Involves both conception and reduction to practice.

Invention date: The U.S. PTO frequently requires inventors to establish dates on which their inventions were made. The inventive act includes both conception and reduction to practice of the invention. For purposes of establishing priority of invention, the date of conception can be used when it is properly established and connected with the reduction to practice. For example, in determining priority of invention, consideration is given not only to date of conception and reduction to practice of the invention, but also to the reasonable diligence of one who was first to conceive and last to reduce to practice, from a time prior to conception by the other. (See *Priority*.)

Joint inventors: In order to constitute two or more persons joint inventors, it is not necessary for the inventive concept to have come to all of them at the same time. It is possible that some of the features may have been contributed by one and other features contributed by all. The only requirement is that the features be so interrelated as to contribute to a unitary result; that is, the contributions of the coinventors must resolve in a patentable combination. The mere doing of routine laboratory or shop work where the exact nature of the work has been outlined by another does not make one an inventor.

License: A waiver of the monopoly granted under a patent whereby the person taking the license (i.e., the licensee) is permitted to practice the invention covered by the patent without liability for infringement of that particular patent.

New matter: Material that involves a departure from, or addition to, the original disclosure; cannot be inserted in an application by amendment or be included in a reissue application. (See *Reissue.*)

Official Action: Communication from the Patent Office to the inventor-applicant setting forth the view of the Office with respect to the patent application as it exists at the time of writing the Action.

Patent: A grant by the United States Government giving an inventor the right to exclude others from making, using, or selling his or her invention within the United States or its territories for a specified period of time (17 years); (does not give the right to practice the invention); patents are also granted by many other countries but do not confer rights as to the invention in the United States.

Patentability: The conditions that must be met before a patent can be granted; generally stated, these conditions are that the patentee:

1. Must make an invention or discovery (see *Invention*).
2. Which must be new.
3. Which must be unobvious.
4. Which must be useful.
5. Which must not have been abandoned (see *Abandonment*).
6. And which must be fully disclosed.

Patentee: The person or persons in whose name the patent is granted. (See *Applicant.*)

Preliminary search: A limited review of the prior art, including patents and publications, made before a patent application is filed to determine whether or not the disclosed invention possesses the requisite of patentability (see *Patentability*); sometimes called a "novelty search" or a "Pre-X." Generally not so exhaustive as that made by the PTO after application is filed; not necessarily a requisite for filing a patent application.

Prior art: The extent of public knowledge as represented by publications or patents in existence and available to the public before the date of the invention. (See *Anticipation*, *Art.*)

Priority: Arises in interference proceeding and refers to "priority of invention." Party must be entitled to award of priority of invention in order to be entitled to patent. Priority belongs to the party who was either the first to conceive and reduce the invention to practice (see *Conception*, *Reduction to Practice*) or, was the first to conceive the invention and proceeded with reasonable diligence (see *Diligence*) to a reduction to practice from a time just prior to the time when his or her opponent entered the field up to the completion of his or her own reduction.

Process: A method, consisting of one or more steps, for producing a new result or for producing an old result in a new way.

Prosecution: The procedures involved in obtaining a patent from the date of filing the patent application to the date of issuance of the patent or abandonment of the application.

Public use: Placing an invention in use for other than experimental purposes without exercising any effective secrecy precautions. (See *Commercial use.*)

Reduction to practice:

Actual :

The physical part of the inventive act; a process is reduced to practice when the series of steps making up the invention are carried out so as to establish the practicability of the process; a composition of matter is reduced to practice when actually produced, unless its usefulness is not apparent, in which event its utility must be demonstrated by actual test; there is "reduction to practice" when a machine or an article of manufacture is embodied in a physical form and its practicability has been demonstrated. The mere act of reduction to practice does not necessarily constitute one a joint inventor. It may be that the invention did not require a physical reduction to practice to establish the practicability of the idea, or the reduction may have been performed by one acting under the direction of the inventor.

Constructive:

The filing of a complete patent application covering the invention.

Reference: Art relied upon for anticipation of an invention. (See *Art*, *Anticipation*, *Prior art.*)

Rejection: A ground upon which the PTO holds the claims unpatentable in their present form. (See *Official Action*, *Amendment*, *Anticipation.*)

Reissue: A statutory remedy permitting a patentee to obtain a substitute patent where his or her original patent is, through error without any deceptive intention, deemed wholly or partly inoperative or invalid by reason of a defective specification or drawing, or by reason of the patentee claiming more or less than he or she had a right to claim in the patent; a reissue patent expires 17 years from date of the original patent; no new matter can be introduced; claims may be broadened by reissue within two years from date of original patent. May also be used to test whether art not considered by the PTO heretofore anticipates the claims in the issued patent. (See *New matter.*)

Response: Applicant's answer, in writing, to an Official Action; may consist solely of arguments or may embody changes to claims, etc. (See *Amendment.*)

Specification: The body portion of a patent application; as generally used, refers to the written description only; technically, it also includes the claims; should contain title of the invention, brief summary of invention, brief description of drawings, if any, and a detailed description of the invention. (See *Application*, *Disclosure*, *Claims*.)

Trade secret: An invention or discovery that may or may not be patentable, and that is used in secrecy without obtaining a patent thereon.

Validity: The acid test that is applied to a patent if it becomes involved in litigation, to determine whether or not the Patent Office was correct in granting such patent; an issued patent carries with it a presumption of validity that can be rebutted by showing that one of the conditions of patentability was lacking at the time when application for the patent was made. (See *Patentability*.)

Index